CHANGING PERSPECTIVES

CHANGING PERSPECTIVES

Christian Culture and Morals in England Today

ROSALIE OSMOND

DARTON·LONGMAN + TODD

First published in 1993 by
Darton, Longman & Todd Ltd
1 Spencer Court
140–142 Wandsworth High Street
London SW18 4JJ

ISBN 0–232–52024–0

A catalogue record for this book is available
from the British Library

Cover: photographs by J. Catling Allen;
design by Judy Linard

Phototypeset by Intype, London
Printed and bound in Great Britain
by Page Bros, Norwich

FOR OLIVER

CONTENTS

PREFACE

The research for this book, including the cost of the survey I commissioned from Gallup Poll, was funded by the Charles Douglas-Home Memorial Trust. I am most grateful to the Trustees and in particular to their chairman, the Hon. Mr Justice Cazalet, for both their financial support and personal encouragement.

I was particularly fortunate to find in Gordon Heald, managing director of Gallup, UK, someone who had a genuine interest in the project and gave help that went well beyond the formal requirements of his contract. His research executive, Emma Brooks, did everything in exemplary fashion, including cheerfully providing numerous extra correlations of data not specified in the original agreement at very short notice.

I am also very grateful to a range of distinguished people who were willing to allow me to interview them. Extracts from a number of these interviews, all of which were recorded, are included in the text. I must thank as well all those anonymous people who were prepared to bare their minds and souls in lengthy sessions to a Gallup interviewer!

My husband has been a great source not only of practical help but of stimulating new perspectives and, through much conversation, has acted as a testing ground for my ideas. My daughter says she and her two brothers must be thanked as well for putting up with me while I was writing it. Actually, I enjoyed the work so much I innocently supposed I was unusually cheerful and accommodating.

INTRODUCTION

This book began as an attempt to discover the extent to which England is still, subliminally at least, culturally and morally Christian. What I was interested in was not 'faith' or 'commitment' as such (about which much of a decidedly gloomy nature has been written), but rather the residual force of knowledge and ideas that were once the property of most educated people in this country. To what extent are our minds still 'supersaturated', to use Joyce's term, with the religion that many of us have rejected?

There are two main elements in the study. The first is a selective examination of literature produced in this country in the last ten years. Literature not only reflects the attitudes of contemporary society but provides an ideal – or counter-ideal – that helps to shape it as well. My interest is not simply in works dealing with religious subjects, such as *Racing Demon* or *Incline our Hearts*, but with what the direction in which the style and structure of modern literature is moving has to say about our perception of reality. As the work progressed, however, it became clear to me that a full investigation of this aspect of the topic could not be achieved within the project's one-year tenure, and that it would demand of the reader a knowledge of literary critical theory incompatible with the rest of the study, which is intended for a more general audience. Therefore, while the literary element remains, it is perhaps less dominant than I had originally imagined it would be.

The second element in the study, on the contrary, expanded successfully beyond my original design. This was a survey, devised by me with the considerable help of Gallup and carried out by that organization, that attempted to measure as objectively as possible attitudes towards and knowledge of Christian culture and morality.

All surveys are, of course, imperfect. You only get answers to the questions you can formulate; you may not always get truthful answers – people seem to have an inexplicable desire to 'appear in a good light' to even the most anonymous pollster. You may get answers that are truthful as far as the respondent is aware, but that are not really thought out. Some of the questions in this survey were complex and may never have occurred to those interviewed before; to expect an intelligent response in a few seconds flat is optimistic, to say the least. Despite these reservations, I am convinced that the survey results are significant and broadly correct. This is particularly true of those that measure objective knowledge rather than subjective opinion. Even in the latter category an immediate response to a question may be 'significant' without being the product of deep thought. The immediate response may well be a more accurate indicator of the values by which the person really acts. The survey falls into two sections: one dealing with 'culture' and one with 'morality'. In each section, there is an attempt to measure attitudes as well as knowledge and to correlate the two.

Those interviewed were not a cross-section of the general population but of three rather élite groups: first-year university students, school teachers, and professionals aged forty to sixty (roughly the right age to be the parents of the students). All had to be born in this country and *not* adherents of a non-Christian religion, though agnostics and atheists were included. In other words, they were people who might reasonably be expected to be familiar with the cultural and moral ethos about which they were being questioned.

Approximately 200 people were interviewed face to face within each group for a total of 614 interviews. A small number of these were chosen for follow-up interviews by myself. Each of the three main groupings was selected so as to give an appropriate spread according to sex, age (except in the case of first-year university students), and geographical location. University students were also divided into three groups according to type of university – Cambridge, three provincial universities (Liverpool, Sheffield, and Bristol), and three polytechnics (Leicester, Newcastle-upon-Tyne, and Kingston). Teachers were drawn from both primary and secondary schools and from the state and independent sectors.

The intention in selecting these 'élite' groups was to produce a 'best possible scenario' of our society, and to focus on those people who are probably most influential in forming public opinion. What these people do not know and value is unlikely to be passed on to future generations.

Surveys purport to be objective. Their interpretation, if it is to be significant, must be set within a context, and that can rarely be completely objective. After the survey results were complete it seemed desirable to share them with various eminent people in fields that related to them and to ask for their reactions. I therefore interviewed at some length a group of such people that included distinguished clerics, a writer, a cathedral organist, a school headmaster, a former member of parliament, and a former newspaper editor. Their views, always perceptive, often witty, sometimes controversial, have been invaluable both in themselves and as a touchstone against which to judge my own reactions.

The structure of the book moves from the individual to the social, and from cultural to moral considerations. The first chapter deals with the issue that seemed key to the need for religion in general and Christianity in particular: a fundamental desire for structure, order, and meaning in the life of the individual. The second chapter looks specifically at the kind of religious experience and worship that is most likely to fulfil this need, and the extent to which (as measured by the survey) people today still have the knowledge that makes it easy for them to respond to traditional patterns of worship and liturgy. Chapter 3 (possibly the most controversial) examines what I perceive to be the mutual distrust that exists between the Church and what one might broadly call 'cultural forces' in our society and suggests some possible reasons for this situation. Chapter 4 looks at attitudes to moral questions as revealed in the survey. The final chapter examines some of the implications of the study's findings for the Church as an institution and for society in this country at large.

The book provides a large number of hard facts satisfyingly bolstered by hard statistics and some rather less hard theories. But in the end, as one might, I suppose, have anticipated, it raises more questions than it answers. How does one reconcile the individual's demonstrable need for pattern and meaning in life (usually seen within a social context) with the quest for individual fulfilment, which, according to the survey, is what most people believe to be the chief purpose of life? How does the Church minister to a people who no longer have the most basic knowledge of the Bible and liturgy, never mind the long tradition of Christian literature and music? And, most difficult of all, how can a religion that has traditionally preached an exclusive faith, 'necessary to salvation', reconcile that with the practical necessities of a peaceful and tolerant life in a multi-cultural society?

I cannot regard unanswered questions as failures. On the contrary, any firm answers I might have proposed from an individual perspective, even backed by the thought and research that has gone into this study, would almost certainly emerge as failures. What I have tried to do is to define the issues as they arise out of the concrete base of both the survey and the literature. One of the depressing things I have become aware of during the past year as I have followed Church news more conscientiously than usual is how much debate – of that reported at least – seems to be focused on inessentials, the periphery of the Church's role. Of course I am also aware (and the survey, if it had done nothing else, would have made me so) that what is essential and what is peripheral are also matters of opinion. Nevertheless, to raise awareness, to set out issues with clarity, should be to sharpen debate and encourage serious thought both within and outside the Church.

1

THE IDEA OF ORDER

Oh! Blessed rage for order, pale Ramon,
The maker's rage to order words of the sea,
Words of the fragrant portals, dimly starred,
And of ourselves and of our origins,
In ghostlier demarcations, keener sounds.
Wallace Stevens, 'The Idea of Order at Key West'

At the heart of human existence lies a profound desire for order. It is so deeply rooted in our nature that it manifests itself at all levels from the mundane, where it is called routine, to the esoteric, where it generates the concrete planning of cities and the abstract systems of theology and philosophy. In sickness it is obsessive-compulsive behaviour providing a false sense of security; in health it is purpose enabling us to function with efficiency and meaning.

It is this sense of purpose that distinguishes the human desire for order from that in animals. For while animals often demonstrate a highly developed sense of order in the organization of their homes and daily lives, in humanity this sense of order takes on a metaphysical dimension. The ordering of the world is perceived as a sign of its purposefulness, its *intention*, rather than its random construction. A sense of order, therefore, is basic to the religious impulse within the individual. This remains true whether we assume that God has created us in his own image, so that we naturally desire to understand and imitate the ordering of creation in our own lives, or whether we assume that, the need for order being a basic human desire, we have constructed a God and a religion that meets this fundamental need.

The early Christian Church was not a highly ordered construct. By its very nature, that of a small sect, following a leader without a permanent base of operations, it could not be. In this it contrasted with the established Jewish religion with its temple, its formal rules of behaviour and worship. The lack of order in early Christianity was associated with the element of risk and daring involved in becoming a member of this new religion. The injunction to 'leave all [including family and friends] and follow me' highlighted this element of uncertainty. In this context it became a positive, not a negative thing. It was a sign of commitment, an indication that believers were so confident in their new-found faith that they no longer needed the props of traditional worship, the emotional support of those formerly closest to them. In the eschatological situation in which the early Christians believed they were living, purpose was found in the promises and prophecies of Christ, which were to be fulfilled imminently. The need for a sustaining structure to support and reinforce a sense of purpose in everyday life, therefore, did not arise; 'everyday life' did not exist; the sense of immediate destiny was too strong.

Only with the legitimization of Christianity under Constantine and the fading of the sense of the imminence of Christ's return did order become an important characteristic of Christianity. It manifested itself in two parallel guises: the structure and government of the Church, and its ritual and liturgy. Within a few hundred years, both of these were established as the dominant features of the medieval Church. It had moved from a loose society with only an elementary organization to one that was conservative and hierarchial. The simple sharing of bread and wine became surrounded by the most structured and ornate liturgies.

These changes were not merely examples of a new religion gradually ossifying and gathering accretions of dubious value. It can be argued that they were the necessary reaction to the recognition that Christianity must settle in for the 'long haul', that it must become a religion for enabling people to live as well as to die. Its extension, both in time and space, necessitated more elaborate structures of government than were essential at first.

The development of the liturgy involved more than this. It served to reinforce both memory and a sense of meaning in those to whom it ministered in the growing Church. As the mass evolved, its propers (assigned readings and special prayers) for half the Church year followed the chief events of the life of Christ. Beginning in Advent with the story of John the Baptist and the preparation for the coming of Christ, it moved through the celebration of his birth at Christmas, his presentation in the temple at Candlemas, his first miracle at Cana, the events leading up to his death and Crucifixion, his Resurrection at Easter, his subsequent appearances to the disciples, and finally his Ascension and the descent of the Holy Spirit at Pentecost. The central act of the mass itself, the consecration of bread and wine and its distribution to the faithful, was an act of memory as well as of sacrifice: 'Do this in remembrance of me'.

The parts of the mass were designed to call to mind certain key events in the life of Christ and theological concepts. The Gloria's echo of the song of the angels to the shepherds, the Creed's rehearsal of the chief acts of each member of the Trinity, the Benedictus' repetition of the crowd's acclamation of Jesus on Palm Sunday – all these, even in a language unfamiliar to a majority of the people, were designed to be a constant reminder of the salient features of Christianity.

Beyond this, however, the developing liturgy was intended to instil a sense of the profound order and significance of Christianity. The constancy of the chief parts of the mass and the unvarying order of the service provided, in a small way, an image of the unchanging order of eternity. Within this the varied but annually recurring cycle of prayers and readings provided an image of the varied but essentially unchanging nature of human existence itself.

In this world nothing was haphazard, nothing was left to chance. Readings from the Old Testament were selected so as to relate prophecy to fulfilment, and an elaborate system of 'correspondences' was read into events in the Old and New Testaments. Thus the rock that Moses struck to produce water in the desert became the pierced side of Christ, gushing water and blood in the New; the ark of Noah became a type of the Church; the manna in the wilderness the bread of the sacrament. These correspondences were not just the property of the erudite. Embodied in stained glass windows and wood carvings they were accessible to the ignorant as well.

The English mystery plays were a natural product of this

mentality. Here the individual correspondences were incorporated into an elaborate dramatic structure that encompassed
the whole history of mankind. These plays, performed by craft
guilds in the Middle Ages, began with the creation of the world
and ended with the Last Judgement. Between these first and
last things lay the sin of Adam and the expulsion from the
garden, the destruction of the world in the flood, the fraternal
struggles of Cain and Abel, of Joseph and his brethren, the
escape from Egypt, all leading to the events of the life of Christ
himself and, beyond that, to the end of the world. It was
possible to stand on a street corner in Chester or Coventry and
see the whole history of the world pass by.

And not only the history of the world. One of the remarkable things about this way of viewing life was that it included
the history of everyman as well. The expulsion of Adam from
the garden was the fall of all human beings into sin at birth;
the crossing of the Red Sea and the eating of the Last Supper
signified their personal redemption from this state. The Last
Judgement, with its separation of the saved from the damned,
depicted not only in the mystery plays but in innumerable
works of art, struck a personal note that it is difficult for
modern people to conceive. These plays showed not only how
things in general came to be; they told the personal history
of the medieval street-corner viewer.

Furthermore, it was not only a history of *what* had happened
and was about to happen; it was an explanation of *why*.
Adam's transgression explained universal sinfulness; universal
sinfulness explained sorrow and suffering – even of those who
were apparently 'good' and 'innocent'. It was not, of course,
a scientific explanation of the sort we would demand today.
But it was comprehensive and teleological. Life did have
meaning; there were rewards and punishments; despite apparent injustices and inequalities, in the end all would be made
right; the righteous would be saved, and the wicked punished
eternally. God himself, who alone knew the secrets of the
heart, would make this judgement. There could be no appeal,
but neither could there be any doubt of its absolute justice.

In addition to the attractiveness of such a comprehensive
explanation of human history and purpose, both the liturgy
and the mystery plays were psychologically satisfying as well.
The Bible stories from which the readings were taken and on

which the plays were based frequently dealt with fundamental human emotions such as sibling rivalry, sexual jealousy, pride, and anger. Just as important as this, however, was the way in which the liturgy, the cycle of the Church year, and the plays catered to the natural rhythm of human emotion with its cycles of despair and rejoicing. The mass began with the Kyrie, asking God to have mercy upon all sinners, followed by the joyous outburst of the Gloria. The prayer of consecration incorporated the acclamation of Jesus as he rode into Jerusalem on Palm Sunday, and the concluding Agnus Dei reiterated the Kyrie's appeal for mercy, but this time on an assured, valedictory note, ending 'Dona nobis pacem' (Grant us thy peace). The structure of the Church year was similarly varied, with the two chief periods of penitence, Advent and Lent, followed by the two major festivals of rejoicing, Christmas and Easter.

As for the mystery plays, in addition to the kinds of psychological realism described above (those based on the subject matter of the Bible stories and those based on the fluctuation of human emotions), they incorporated the more mundane realism of natural speech and humour. No one who has read or seen the *Second Shepherd's Play* from the Coventry cycle or *Noye's Fludde* (either in its original or Britten's operatic version) can forget the cunning deception of Max, the sheep stealer, or the comic, pig-headed disobedience of Noah's wife and her 'gossips'. One of the great achievements of these plays is the way in which they combine humour and seriousness of purpose and, in this respect, provide a model for later English drama, both comic and tragic. Comprehensive, realistic (on many levels), and teleological, they were ambitious and, one assumes from their popularity, satisfying to their audiences in a way that has seldom been surpassed.

If then the desire for order has been fundamental to the human race, at least as it has developed in the western Judeo-Christian tradition, and if the Church and its various cultural accretions have been ideally designed to satisfy that need, what about the present day? Does the need still exist, have we lost it, or have we found other ways of satisfying it?

For some of the devout the old forms and patterns are unquestionably still effective. When I talked to Michael

Mayne, Dean of Westminster, he spoke of the need for structure as one of the great secrets of the success of the monastic orders, and the way in which they provide a link 'at once with the whole historical tradition' as well as 'a world-wide tradition'. The links are thus both vertical and lateral. 'You're connected with the whole living tradition from the past and you're connected with what your brothers and sisters are doing throughout the world.'

But what of a cross-section of intelligent adults from various walks of life? It was the needs and reactions of these people that the survey that has formed the basis of this study attempted to discover. The survey showed clearly that the need for order does still exist, though it is less easy to define precisely what it comprises and how it is perceived to be satisfied.

One of the key questions asked was 'Some say that life forms a meaningful pattern while others think life is just a chance series of events with no meaning. Which of these two beliefs comes closest to your own view?' Overall, 58% of the sample replied 'a meaningful pattern'; 30% 'a chance series of events'; 11% on their own initiative said 'a mixture of these'. When the question returned in a slightly different and stronger form later in the survey the response in favour of life having meaning was even more pronounced. Faced with the statement 'Life has no purpose or meaning', only 3% agreed strongly, with another 3% 'tending to agree'; 17% tended to disagree, and 69% 'strongly disagreed'.

It would seem that in general people believe, or at least wish to believe, that life has meaning, although a very significant minority do not share this view. Further, Table 1 shows that the perception that life has meaning correlates positively with seeing oneself as Christian rather than agnostic or atheist, with education at a church-affiliated state school and, within those who consider themselves Christian, it correlates positively with commitment as measured by frequency of church attendance.

But the bald statistics raise as many questions as they answer. Does Christianity encourage people to see life as a meaningful pattern, or are people who need to see life in this way particularly drawn to Christianity? Or, as is most likely, do the two reinforce one another?

Of the three main groupings in the survey, students are least likely to see life as a meaningful pattern, and teachers are most likely to do so. The fact that there is only one percentage point difference between teachers and professionals would seem to indicate that the difference between both these groups and the students is a function of age rather than of occupation. What the statistics cannot reveal is whether the students, in their turn, will come to see life as having a pattern as they grow older or whether we are witnessing a genuine change in attitude that will be permanent in our society. Only a follow-up survey of the same group in twenty years' time could provide a definitive answer to this question, but it seems likely that, to some extent at least, this change is real, not simply apparent. General changes in social and philosophical thinking discussed below would reinforce this trend and make this point of view probable.

Those surveyed were also asked to agree or disagree with a series of more specific statements about their attitudes to life and death. These were designed to probe the values by which they lived, their 'philosophy of life'. In answer to the statements that focused specifically on the meaning and purpose of life, the largest positive response was obtained to the proposal that 'The main purpose of life is to fulfil yourself'. Overall, 32% of the sample 'agreed strongly' with this statement, and 45% 'tended to agree'. Here again, it was the students who led the way; 46% of them agreed strongly with this statement, and 40% 'tended to agree' – an 86% positive response. For schoolteachers the figures were 26% and 48% and for professionals 23% and 47%. Thus not only was the overall positive response greater for the students, but the strength of agreement was even more notable. The answers to this question correlated inversely with those dealing with life as meaningful and patterned. People who saw life as a meaningful pattern were *less* likely to agree with the statement than those who saw it as a chance series of events (3.74 and 4.12 mean scores respectively, rated on a scale of 1 to 5), and the mean score also correlated negatively, in a satisfyingly graduated pattern, from 'Christian' through 'agnostic' to 'atheist' and also with Christian commitment as measured by church attendance (see Table 2).[1]

This question was closely followed in degree of positive

TABLE 1 *Meaning and purpose of life (col. %)*

	SAMPLE GROUP				SEX		SUBJECTS				QUALIFICATIONS				POLITICS		SEES LIFE AS	
	Total	Stud-ents	Teach-ers	Profes-sionals	Male	Female	Scien-ces	Appl. Scien-ces	Arts	Vocat-ional	Post grad.	Degree	Dip-loma/ 'A' level	Other	Left	Right	Mean-ingful patt.	Chance series of events
Total	614	205	214	195	388	226	159	88	188	198	136	319	141	17	253	298	357	183

Some say that life forms a meaningful pattern while others think life is just a chance series of events with no meaning. Which of these two beliefs comes closest to your own view?

A meaningful pattern	58	50	63	62	56	62	60	59	60	60	59	58	59	59	54	61	100	–
A chance series of events	30	38	24	27	32	25	27	33	29	29	27	31	30	24	32	30	–	100
A mixture of these	11	11	11	10	10	12	11	7	9	11	13	9	11	18	11	9	–	–

How often, if at all, do you think about the meaning and purpose of life?

Often	44	37	45	51	45	43	42	40	52	45	54	43	38	35	51	40	53	28
Sometimes	40	42	43	35	37	45	37	41	37	40	35	39	43	59	35	42	39	40
Rarely	14	19	13	11	15	12	18	17	10	14	11	14	18	6	13	15	8	26
Never	2	2	–	3	3	*	3	2	2	1	1	3	1	–	1	2	–	5
Don't know	*	*	–	–	*	–	1	–	–	–	–	*	–	–	–	*	–	1

	Total	DENOMINATION				BELIEF			RELIGIOUS UPBRINGING		RELIGIOUS ATTENDANCE				SCHOOLING			
		Cath-olic	C. of E.	Metho-dist	None	Chris-tian	Agno-stic	Athe-ist	Yes	No	Once week or more	Once month	Less often	Never	Non-den. state	Church-aff. state	Non-den. indep.	Church-aff. indep.
Total	614	60	350	76	94	385	142	78	332	281	161	87	192	174	371	70	93	79

Some say that life forms a meaningful pattern while others think life is just a chance series of events with no meaning. Which of these two beliefs comes closest to your own view?

	Total	Cath-olic	C. of E.	Metho-dist	None	Chris-tian	Agno-stic	Athe-ist	Yes	No	Once week or more	Once month	Less often	Never	Non-den. state	Church-aff. state	Non-den. indep.	Church-aff. indep.
A meaningful pattern	58	68	59	71	29	74	35	24	65	50	91	70	45	36	57	70	56	58
A chance series of events	30	17	30	17	54	16	49	65	22	39	3	16	41	49	33	17	24	30
A mixture of these	11	15	11	11	12	9	15	8	12	9	6	14	13	12	8	13	19	11

How often, if at all, do you think about the meaning and purpose of life?

	Total	Cath-olic	C. of E.	Metho-dist	None	Chris-tian	Agno-stic	Athe-ist	Yes	No	Once week or more	Once month	Less often	Never	Non-den. state	Church-aff. state	Non-den. indep.	Church-aff. indep.
Often	44	53	39	43	47	47	43	31	46	42	63	44	34	37	44	53	40	44
Sometimes	40	33	43	37	40	40	38	42	42	37	32	48	43	40	39	31	46	43
Rarely	14	13	15	17	12	11	18	19	11	18	4	6	21	20	15	14	14	8
Never	2	–	2	3	1	1	1	6	2	2	1	2	2	3	2	1	–	5
Don't know	*	–	*	–	–	–	–	1	–	*	–	–	1	–	*	–	–	–

* Less than 0.5

TABLE 2 *Attitude statements towards life and death* (col. %)

	SAMPLE GROUP				SEX		SUBJECTS				QUALIFICATIONS				POLITICS		SEES LIFE AS	
	Total	Students	Teachers	Professionals	Male	Female	Sciences	Appl. Sciences	Arts	Vocational	Post grad.	Degree	Diploma/'A' level	Other	Left	Right	Meaningful patt.	Chance series of events
Total	614	205	214	195	388	226	159	88	188	198	136	319	141	17	253	298	357	183
The main purpose of life is to fulfil yourself																		
Strongly agree (+5)	32	46	26	23	28	38	23	39	38	27	26	36	26	35	29	30	30	35
Tend to agree (+4)	45	40	48	47	47	41	46	41	43	48	47	41	53	35	46	47	43	49
Neither nor (+3)	8	7	9	7	7	8	9	6	5	9	7	8	7	18	8	7	7	9
Tend to disagree (+2)	10	5	12	13	11	8	15	7	9	10	11	10	10	–	13	8	12	5
Strongly disagree (+1)	5	2	5	9	6	5	6	8	5	5	9	4	4	12	4	8	8	2
Don't know	*	–	*	1	1	–	1	–	–	–	–	*	1	–	*	–	–	1
Mean score	3.88	4.21	3.80	3.62	3.81	4.00	3.64	3.95	4.01	3.83	3.71	3.96	3.88	3.82	3.85	3.82	3.74	4.12

	DENOMINATION				BELIEF			RELIGIOUS UPBRINGING		RELIGIOUS ATTENDANCE				SCHOOLING			
	Total	Cath-olic	C. of E.	Metho-dist	None	Chris-tian	Agno-stic	Athe-ist	Yes	No	Once week or more	Once month	Less often	Never	Non-den. state	Church-aff. state	Non-den. indep.	Church-aff. indep.
Total	614	60	350	76	94	385	142	78	332	281	161	87	192	174	371	70	93	79

The main purpose of life is to fulfil yourself

	Total	Cath-olic	C. of E.	Metho-dist	None	Chris-tian	Agno-stic	Athe-ist	Yes	No	Once week or more	Once month	Less often	Never	Non-den. state	Church-aff. state	Non-den. indep.	Church-aff. indep.
Strongly agree (+5)	32	42	32	25	37	28	37	41	30	35	19	29	34	43	30	39	35	29
Tend to agree (+4)	45	45	46	46	43	45	46	42	46	43	41	49	50	41	45	43	44	46
Neither nor (+3)	8	8	9	7	4	8	8	8	7	9	6	9	9	7	8	9	4	11
Tend to disagree (+2)	10	3	9	17	10	12	4	6	11	8	24	7	5	4	9	6	15	10
Strongly disagree (+1)	5	2	5	5	4	7	4	1	6	5	11	6	2	3	7	4	1	4
Don't know	*	–	–	–	2	–	1	1	*	*	–	–	–	1	1	–	–	–
Mean score	3.88	4.22	3.91	3.68	4.01	3.74	4.11	4.17	3.83	3.95	3.32	3.89	4.09	4.17	3.83	4.06	3.98	3.86

* Less than 0.5

response by the hedonistic 'The main purpose of life is to gain enjoyment from it', but here, as one might expect, the results correlate even more negatively with church affiliation and religious commitment. Of atheists 36% 'strongly agree' while only 18% of agnostics and 14% of Christians do so. Among Christians it is the Catholics who are most able to see 'enjoyment' as compatible with religion (23% 'strongly agree'), while among the ranks of the Nonconformists only 8% do so. Even more significant, however, is the negative correlation between this question and the one about pattern and meaning in life. Of those who see life as a meaningful pattern, only 15% 'strongly agree' that its main purpose is to enjoy yourself; among those who see it as a 'chance series of events' 28% (nearly twice as many) do so.

We appear to be dealing here with two contrary impulses in our society – the social and the individualistic. To see life as a pattern is normally to see one's own destiny as part of some larger whole. To see the end of life as individual fulfilment or enjoyment does not imply anything outside the bounds of oneself. Yet the high percentage of agreement with all three statements (that life is a meaningful pattern and that life is about fulfilling yourself and/or gaining enjoyment) would seem to indicate that many people want both; the lack of positive correlation between the first and the last two shows, however, that they are not inherently compatible values; there is a tension between them.

We cannot go further without examining more closely what 'life as a meaningful pattern' may connote. While the historical context in which I have set the idea here is a social one, and the use of the word 'pattern' in the questionnaire presumably suggested, as it was meant to, that idea in the respondents, there are other possibilities. And while the straight hedonism of 'enjoying yourself' is manifestly incompatible with traditional Christianity, with self-fulfilment the case is not so clear cut. It is not impossible to see life as a highly individual construct, yet meaningful and 'patterned' to the particular person involved. Indeed, the tradition of Protestant, Nonconformist thought and writing is very much along these lines. The corporate, social pattern of meaning that was prevalent in the Catholic Church and is essentially what I have described in the early part of this chapter was lost at the time of the Reformation in favour of a view of life as a personal, individualistic pilgrimage. Although it can be argued that the second part of *Pilgrim's Progress* depicts, through Christiana and her children, the progress of the whole Church to the Celestial City, the dominant impression of the book is of the lonely figure, Christian, occasionally succoured on his journey by a companion such as Faithful, but essentially responsible for his own fate, making his journey in isolation through a forbidding and hostile landscape.

The primacy of the individual conscience, the emphasis on faith, which is unseen, rather than works, which can be seen, led to an internalization of religion and meaning. There are those, notably Durkheim, who argue that there is a clear connection between Christianity and the modern 'deification of the individual'. It is 'incorrect to present the individualistic ethic as the antagonist of Christian morality. Quite the contrary – the former derived from the latter.'[2]

If it were simply this phenomenon we were encountering in this survey, however, we would expect to find that Nonconformists scored higher on both questions (seeing life as a meaningful pattern and feeling that the chief purpose of life is to fulfil yourself) – in other words, that there was a significant overlap within this group in the responses to both questions. But this is not the case. While Nonconformists score slightly higher than Catholics on the first question (71% and 68% respectively), it is Catholics who are much more likely to see the chief purpose of life as being to fulfil yourself (42% of Catholics and 25% of Nonconformists 'strongly agree'). The most positive response to this question that measures an individualistic approach to life comes, therefore, from that group which, in religious terms at least, has been unaffected by the Reformation, and the internalization of conscience and rise of individualism that it inspired.

Another statement in this part of the survey asserts that 'Life is meaningful only because of the existence of God'. Here one finds that 33% of Catholics 'agree strongly', in contrast to only 16% of Nonconformists (the mean scores are 3.62 and 3.20 respectively). Linking this response to those relating to individual fulfilment further erodes the idea that we are dealing here with a traditional Protestant response to life that combines meaning with highly individualistic goals. Within

Christianity it is those who adhere to the corporate structures of Catholicism that are more likely to see life as meaningful only because of the existence of God, and who are also more likely to believe that the chief purpose of life is to fulfil yourself. It would seem then that what we have here are two inherently contradictory impulses, possibly not fully recognized and certainly not resolved by the respondents, who want both corporate meaning and individual fulfilment in their lives. The responses of the students (lower than average perception of life as a meaningful pattern and higher than average belief that life is about self-fulfilment) show that there is a generational movement away from corporate pattern and towards individual satisfaction. Only 9% of students strongly agree that 'Life is meaningful only because of the existence of God' in contrast to 21% of teachers and professionals.

When one comes to the most extremely 'religious' and also individualistic option within this general question about the meaning of life, 'Life is mainly a preparation for death and an afterlife', one finds an even less positive response. Only 6% overall 'strongly agreed' with this statement, while 15% 'tended to agree'; 64% either 'strongly disagreed' or 'tended to disagree'. As one might expect with a statement demanding such a specifically 'committed' response there is a significant difference between those who attended church-affiliated state or independent schools and those whose education was non-denominational: 10% who attended church schools 'strongly agree' while only 5% and 4% who attended non-denominational state or independent schools do so. Again, it is Roman Catholics who are most likely to agree strongly with this statement (22% as against 3% for Church of England and 7% for Nonconformists). Yet this is precisely the view of life that was prevalent in early seventeenth-century England among the Puritans. Thus William Crashaw could state as the merest commonplace in his introduction to his translation of the *Visio Philiberti*: 'The end, and highest happiness of a Christian man, is to honour God in this life, and to die well.'[3] Clearly, the hard-line religious response has undergone a shift and is no longer generally typical of Nonconformist religion.

This refusal to see life as a preparation for death and an afterlife ties in with the high level of agreement with the statement 'Death is inevitable; it is pointless to worry about it'. Altogether an astonishing 88% either strongly agree (53%) or 'tend to agree' (35%) with this question. Further, the response is surprisingly uniform across religious denominations and among believers and unbelievers. Atheists agree in even greater numbers than Christians, but agnostics, on the other hand, are marginally less likely to 'agree strongly' than their Christian counterparts. One can surely assume, therefore, that the notion of the Christian life as a testing ground, a probationary period for what comes afterwards, is well and truly dead. The demise of a belief in hell (according to Gallup's recent *Values* survey, only 25% of people any longer believe in its existence) may not be entirely coincidental either. The response to this statement about death also provides further confirmation that the type of individualism we are dealing with here is *not* in a direct line of descent from that of the Protestant reformers.

The survey provided one alternative that was both secular and corporate rather than individualistic: 'The main purpose of life is procreation and continuity'. Here the rate of agreement was surprisingly low. Only 10% overall 'strongly agreed', and 27% 'tended to agree' for a mean score of 2.96. Atheists, as one would expect, were more likely to agree than Christians (17% 'strongly agreed' as against 10%), but rather strangely, agnostics were less likely to 'strongly agree' than either group (6%). Even more inexplicably, there is a negative correlation between the response to this question and seeing life as a meaningful pattern. Thus it would seem that in this age when much of the emphasis of modern secular movements, such as that concerned with ecology, is on the kind of world we leave to our children and to mankind in general, this does not provide a sufficiently strong motivating force within individuals to enable them to see their lives as 'meaningful or patterned'. Individualism appears to triumph over even a secular purpose that is collective and corporate.

When asked whether 'sorrow and suffering have purpose within a larger pattern', however, more than half the respondents either 'agree strongly' or 'tend to agree'. This gives confirmation within a specific context of the general tendency to see life as a 'meaningful pattern' rather than a 'chance series of events'. There is a significant correlation with religious commitment, and within Christian denominations it is again

the Catholics who are most likely to agree and the Nonconformists who are least likely. What one is forced to ask (and
cannot definitively answer) is whether this represents the *conviction* that life does, in the end, make sense, or merely the
pious hope or desperate need to assert that it does so. Which-
ever is the case it does seem to point again to at least the
desire to perceive life as having meaning in the face of a
strong contrary pull towards an individualistic and hedonistic
philosophy of life.

The growth of extreme individualism, which seeks for
meaning only within the parameters of the self, and which
has been exacerbated in England in the last decade by economic and social policies, is reinforced by certain modern
theologies and literary theories. In both fields there has been
a profound questioning of the 'received' ideas of the past. In
popular theology in England this phenomenon began with the
publication of *Honest to God* by John Robinson in the early
sixties and has surfaced most recently in the controversy sur-
rounding the remarks of the Bishop of Durham about the
literal truth of the Resurrection.

It is not my purpose to evaluate the merits of these theological debates. Their effect, however, does bear directly on my
subject. In general, this effect (even on quite well-educated
and intelligent churchgoers) seems to have been to call into
question certain beliefs they had considered absolute articles
of the faith without replacing them with anything else of
substance to which they can adhere. This does not mean that
the theologians are wrong or that, even if they are right, they
would have done well to keep their mouths shut. Rather it
seems to show that people who are willing to take the trouble
to understand quite sophisticated arguments in other areas of
life (science or politics, for example) are unwilling to do so in
relation to religion. Thus the Resurrection must be either
'true' or 'not true'. If any detail of the biblical account is
questioned, the whole moves automatically into the category
of 'not true'.

Some of the fault may also lie with the Church itself and
its presentation of these arguments. Very few clergy and bishops seem to credit the laity with the ability and/or the willing-
ness to enter into theological debate. Things must be kept
simple. At the heart of much preaching and religious teaching

lies a terrible condescension. In some cases one suspects the clergy themselves are threatened by the new theology that 'calls all in doubt', and feel compelled to reject it out of hand in self-defence.

Far beyond anything suggested by the Bishop of Durham (or anyone else within the bounds of orthodoxy, for that matter) lies the theology of Don Cupitt. The author of such titles as *Taking Leave of God* has moved totally away from Christianity as a religion that is objectively 'true' to one that is 'true' because it satisfies certain essential human needs and desires. He has said, 'I no longer believe there is any "capital T" Truth of the sort that Plato was after. I'm happy to accept that we live in a culture of signs and stories. It's up to each of us to make something of our own.'[4] The question that I raised in passing at the beginning of this chapter as to whether religion comes from God or man is here answered: it comes from man but nevertheless holds the same central and imperative place in our lives as if it came from a god. Objective truth becomes an irrelevant criterion of value, which is derived instead from the 'usefulness' of religion in enabling us to lead full and satisfying lives. 'God is the mythical embodiment of all that one is concerned with in the spiritual life. . . He is needed – but as a myth.'[5]

This position raises certain interesting questions apart from the obvious one of whether anyone holding these views can still legitimately be called 'Christian'. Are all adherents of the Church to be initiated into the very sophisticated thought processes that support Don Cupitt's arguments and into the means of creating their own sustaining stories, or do we end up with two classes of people – the myth creators and the myth believers? Don Cupitt's own assumption seems to be that all are capable of becoming myth creators. Indeed, he inveighs against the 'class society' that has, as its most unjustifiable result, 'the imparity of consciousness that seems inseparable from [it].'[6] Even if the initiation of all is an attainable ideal, however, it still raises the question as to whether those who are thus initiated, the myth creators, can be 'saved' by their own myth. Can a fiction, once it is consciously known to be a fiction, still work its magic? The people who watched the mystery plays pass by their street corner in Chester six hundred years ago *believed* in the essential veracity of what they saw passing in front of them; but so did those who put on the plays; so did those who wrote them. Can a religion where objectivity has been so completely eroded remain the sustaining and life-giving source that Don Cupitt seems to imagine it can?

The Church today is no longer the repository of order and meaning that it once was. Many would say 'And a very good thing, too'. Again, Don Cupitt: 'Our culture has assigned to Christianity the task of guarding tradition and being the repository of admittedly obsolete but deeply cherished beliefs and images. The church is a museum. . .'[7] While some seek to shake it out of this perceived status, others lament that it is no longer a very effective museum; the curators have defaulted. What is indisputable is that it is no longer well-equipped to provide a counterbalance to the forces of individualism in modern society.

If modern theology has questioned the orthodoxies of the past so, within its own sphere, has literary theory. The connection between the two may not be immediately apparent, yet it is in the kind of stories that we tell in any age that we find one of the most profound clues to the kind of people we are, the things we value, and the perception of reality we hold. The mystery plays, to which I keep returning, were 'true' but were 'stories'. If literature is an imitation of life, perhaps we can see most clearly what we are by looking steadily at that imitation which, in its turn, provides us with a model on which to base life. The relationship is a two-way one. 'Man is in his actions and practice, as well as in his fictions, essentially a story-telling animal. He is not essentially, but becomes through his history, a teller of stories that aspire to truth.'[8]

In the past literature's imitation of life has consisted of a selection, a shaping, a pointing of direction, a clarification. We know more fully what happened to Oedipus the King or Macbeth than what has happened to ourselves because of this pointing of emphasis, this economy that ruthlessly cuts out everything that does not move towards the final revelation. And there *is* a final revelation. We expect one; it is why we have gone to the theatre, opened the covers of the book. We don't particularly care whether the lives we watch or read about are happy or sad; what we require is that they are interesting and that they 'go somewhere'. In some cases (as in the novels of Dickens) this sense of progress is linked to a sense of justice – whether divine or human – but this is not a universal or necessary requirement. What *is* required is the sense of shaping that seems often so perilously absent from our own lives but that (perhaps for that very reason) we seek in fictional ones. It is almost an act of faith as if we believe (or used to believe) that life is or should be like that, and seek to discern in its 'imitation' patterns that we may extrapolate into our own existence. We say this literature is 'realistic', but it has been inherently idealistic as well in showing us clearly patterns and connections that are only dimly visible in everyday life.

In recent years all this has changed. Much modern literature quite deliberately eschews 'pattern' in the traditional sense. Of course, it may be argued that as early as Chekhov one is dealing with literature that no longer fulfils the expectations of the reader brought up on the traditional nineteenth-century novel. But Chekhov's characters at least believe life *could* be purposeful; they *fail* to get to Moscow. In much of modern literature the equivalent of Moscow simply does not exist.

The more extreme versions may portray events that are apparently random simply because 'this is the way life is'. Here a naive realism has triumphed and all elements of idealism have disappeared. Alternatively, there is an 'arrangement', but one designed not according to any pattern that the author sees as intrinsic in life but according to an arbitrary one that the writer (or narrator) imposes on it. Or, in yet another variation, the author deliberately charges the reader with the responsibility for deducing any order or significance from the narrative being related. When Don Cupitt talks about our living in a 'culture of signs and stories' he is speaking deliberately out of a knowledge of recent literary theory. Signs and symbols are what we live by, but they are both conventional and arbitrary – that is, the conventions have no *necessary* foundation in reality.

One of the most recent examples of a literary work based on the consistent but arbitrary use of signs and symbols is the acclaimed novel *Immortality* by Kundera in which a particular gesture, a wave of farewell, recurs in different characters and situations throughout the novel as a motif not wholly dissimilar to Proust's use of the musical motif, but more self-consciously artificial. The novel deals with large questions, and promises much, as its very title indicates. And if I say that, in the end, despite the stylistic brilliancy, it remains episodic and does not live up to its title, I am probably revealing more about traditional expectations than about Kundera's success or lack of it in his own terms.

These works of literature are still 'imitations of life': they simply see the life they are imitating differently from writers of the past. And just as that earlier literature, through its presentation of pattern and meaning in fictional lives, encouraged us to look for similar structures in our own, so these modern works discourage any such attempt. Indeed, there is a sense among some writers that looking for such patterns is itself a naive and child-like activity, a carry-over from childhood or the religious past. 'If I had been younger, I would have figured out a story', says the narrator in 'The Stone in the Field', a short story by the Canadian writer Alice Munro. Where authors such as Kundera do 'figure out' connections and patterns (if not stories) there is no pretence that these patterns are anything other than self-created; they do not correspond to any external or objective 'reality'; as such they are the literary equivalents of the Don Cupitt brand of religion.

In writers such as Alan Ayckbourn the 'figuring out' seems almost a substitute for meaning. The exceptional intricacy of the plots of such plays as *The Norman Conquests* appear as a desperate ploy against the vacancy of the lives they portray. Patterns of connection and coincidence give an *illusion* of significance. This illusion would seem to be deliberate on Ayckbourn's part; he himself has no false notions of his characters' importance. It is rather *their* need to reinvent their lives that is explored.

Margaret Drabble's novel *The Radiant Way* presents an almost textbook example of the progression from pattern and meaning to entertaining episode and implicitly questions the whole notion of an objective order in life. The title, which is taken, as we discover, from a children's reading primer, suggests life as a clear path leading, through increasing knowledge and experience, to some luminous goal. But within the novel it is also used by Charles, husband of one of the three main characters, as the ironic title of a television documentary intending to show the deficiencies of English state schools in Britain in the sixties. And years later Charles' view of education (still meaningful even if with the inverted meaning of irony) is revised in a further television programme made by his son. This is a work with no particular point of view about life at 'an expensive, sporty, minor public school'. It shows 'a crowd of upper-middle-class twits making fools of themselves for the entertainment of the nation. . .' Jonathan claims it is social satire; Alan, his brother, retorts that 'Jonathan's own position was neither objective nor satiric, but simply vacuous, timeserving, frivolous. . .'[9] Liz, his mother, agrees that the film is 'curiously unfocused in intent if not in image, its mocking, tongue-in-cheek evocations of privilege and prejudice curiously flattering to viewer and subject: For Amusement Only, it seemed to say' (p. 299).

The structure of the novel as a whole is that of consecutive episodes from the lives of the three protagonists, interweaving, yet separate. There is no lack of incident, and one of the women, Alix, would seem to believe it may all mean something given that she wants 'Say not the Struggle Nought Availeth' sung at her funeral. But the 'struggle' itself seems to be fragmented, not just among the characters, but within each of them.

In the sequential novel, *A Natural Curiosity*, there is much talk of 'meaning', but no real ability to decipher it. Visions of completeness occur but cannot be sustained – perhaps because they must be self-generated, having no place in the culture as a whole. Charles is described as 'Modern Man, programmed to take in several story lines, several plots at once. He cannot quite unravel them, but he cannot do without the conflicting impulses, the disparate stimuli'.[10] And this is his ex-wife, Liz, momentarily distracted from her work as a psychiatrist:

> She tries to think of the whole human race, on its quest for its own self and its own destruction. The death instinct. For a moment, she encompassed it, she saw it for what it was, in its whole cycle, but then lost it again,

her vision failed her, she shrank and sank back into her body, into her consulting room, into her contemplation of the letters on her desk. (p. 212)

Esther too desires to know 'truth', to understand what life is about. It is part of why she devotes herself to visiting Paul Whitmore, a serial murderer:

He is like a theorem. When she has measured him, she will know the answer to herself and to the whole matter. The Nature of Man, Original Sin, Evil and Good. It is all to be studied there, in captive P. Whitmore. . . (p. 5)

But the theorem is never completely unravelled, and the attempt to give Paul's savagery an historical perspective by linking it to that of the ancient Britons doesn't really work in any universal way. This does not have to be seen as a failure. On the contrary, Esther can welcome the *lack* of certainty in life:

One would think . . . that at our age things would be *clearer*. That life, if you like, would be even *more* circular than it is. That options would have diminished to nothingness. Instead of opening up. As they do. (p. 306)

When I spoke to Margaret Drabble about the demise of traditional structures she admitted the change and acknowledged the vision of uncertainty as her own. 'The modern or postmodern experience of history has led us to see less shape; the concept of progress as being a tidy movement towards enlightenment . . . is no longer tidy as it seemed to be, and I certainly believe that my own fiction reflects that sense of insecurity of purpose. . .' Yet she remains optimistic. 'We've got to say, "Yes, the future is more exciting!" We can't just retreat into mumbo jumbo.' We should have the courage to move on and create our own new structures.

This was all very well in theory, I argued, but how many of us are capable of the intellectual and emotional effort (not to say the sheer ability) this requires? Are we back to the division between the myth creators and the myth believers?

There are, of course, exceptional people (and writers are likely to feature largely among them) who apparently do succeed in creating their own order and structures according to

which to live their lives. At the other end of the spectrum –
and perhaps this is the key to those who seem to espouse no
views, either traditional or modern – there are people who do
not seem to need to think about the meaning and purpose of
life at all. In answer to the question 'How often, if at all, do
you think about the meaning and purpose of life?' 44% overall
replied 'often', 40% 'sometimes', 14% 'rarely', and a bold
2% 'never'. The percentage of those replying 'often' increased
directly with the level of education, ranging from 35% of those
with no degree or diploma qualifications to 53% among those
with postgraduate training – some slim proof, perhaps, that
education does encourage thought in the broad sense of the
word. The young (first-year university students) again showed
up less well than their professional elders. Christians were
significantly more likely to reply 'often' than either agnostics
or atheists, thereby giving the lie to the notion that Christianity is the option of the accepting non-thinker. Less easy to
explain is the discrepancy between Roman Catholics, Anglicans, and Nonconformists. Among the Catholics 53% claimed
they thought 'often' about the meaning of life as compared to
43% of Nonconformists and a mere 39% of Anglicans. The
figure for the latter can be explained by the large number of
nominal Christians that are included in the grouping of an
established church, but the significant discrepancy between
the Roman Catholics and Nonconformists I shall leave their
respective church leaders to ponder!

In the course of my follow-up interviews, I chose to talk to
one of the professionals who claimed not to think about the
meaning of life with any great frequency and who also saw
life as a chance series of events rather than as a 'meaningful
pattern'. For the sake of tidiness, I wish I could record that
he was a psychological wreck, embittered and unhappy, but
nothing could be further from the truth. Highly intelligent
and successful in two quite different and successive careers,
husband of one wife, father of loved children, he seemed
eminently well-adjusted. Indeed, his remarks suggested that
the desire for pattern in life was a weakness, the result of some
deficiency. 'Maybe there are others who are less fortunate and
need to fall back on some underlying pattern.' When I asked
him if he had never made up stories about himself and his
life he denied it with the diffidence of one to whom such an

idea had never occurred. 'I don't think I'm a story-telling person.' Did other people do these things, he wondered. He had no religious affiliation and desired none. Happy in his children, he nevertheless disclaimed any desire to see them carrying on his interests and occupations.

This is clearly an exceptional individual, and even he, while seeing life as a 'series of chance events', rejected the more extreme 'Life has no purpose or meaning', as did all but 3% of those surveyed. As Margaret Drabble said, 'If one believed in total randomness it would be very hard to get up in the morning. . . Life is a suspension of disbelief.'

Most people, however, choose not to acknowledge it as a suspension of disbelief, even if it actually is. Whether or not one can subscribe to the meaning assigned to it by traditional Christianity, there is a deep-seated need to feel that *some* meaning does exist – and that it is real, objective, not just self-created, an illusion of the imagination. Life must be like a story; a story is what best reflects life.

This notion, even in the face of overwhelming evidence to the contrary, is well illustrated in a recent short story, 'Devil's Thumb', published in the *New Yorker*. The chaotic life of Dixie, through whose consciousness the story unfolds, is contrasted with that of the heroines in the stories by 'Treat Redheart' to which she is addicted. These books appear to be Harlequin-romance type products, and at one level she knows life (at least her life) isn't like that and isn't likely to become like that. Yet she still longs for the clear progression of life in the romances, the certainty that all will be well in the end. It proves a vain hope. At the conclusion of the story Dixie is sitting up in bed surrounded by crumpled clothes and thinking about her laundry that got locked up in the laundromat on the previous day while she drank herself into oblivion in the local pub:

> three machines full of wet laundry that someone will take out and pile somewhere, so it will fall on the floor and get dirty all over again, and she knows this can't be right. If there's a definite plan before you're born – all those steps toward getting you into life – there must be a plan for once you're in it, and something is blocking her

plan. . . A life should go toward something, the way life does in Treat Redheart's books. It should go forward.[11]

Dixie finds her simplistic desire for order and meaning fed by the romances of a tenth-rate writer. But, as we have seen, much of the literature of the past has also catered to just this basic, if unsophisticated, desire. The great writers of the early part of this century – Joyce, Woolf, Eliot – all used the history and literature of previous ages as devices to give added resonance and structure to their works. ('These fragments I have shored against my ruins.') It is a curious paradox of the past decade that, while much of our literature for the first time in history requires little or no knowledge of past history or writing to be comprehensible, some, and among that some of the best, returns again in a very self-conscious way to writers of the past for inspiration and structure. *Flaubert's Parrot* and *Possession* are two works that spring immediately to mind, but they are by no means isolated examples. Further, a surprising number of novels written in this country in the last decade show a return to the conventional in plot and outlook. They are not teleological in the sense that the epic was teleological; they do not necessarily claim great importance for their subjects or their fate, but in a modest way they tell a story. They at least pretend to 'go somewhere'.

Going further than this, there are still those writers who believe that fiction ought to deal with ideas, ought to be significant. Resigning from his position as a judge of the Booker prize, Nicholas Mosley wrote: 'I still think there is a job that only novels can do, which is to discover and portray patterns in life that can be conveyed in no better way.'[12]

The rejection of traditional religion does not automatically involve the rejection of pattern and meaning. Indeed, many of the new theories of human nature and society in the nineteenth and early twentieth centuries (Darwinism, Freudianism, Marxism and sociology) were in part 'substitutes for Christian and Aristotelian cosmologies'. They were 'a response to personal and collective needs for symbolic order and meaning in the face of the enfeeblement of the Judaeo-Christian tradition.'[13]

Literature itself can be (and has been) elevated into a kind of pseudo-religion. The quotation at the head of this chapter is from a poem (and a poet) intent on doing precisely that. It is words and music and their arrangement that order Wallace Stevens' world in 'The Idea of Order at Key West'. 'She [the singer] was the single artificer of the world/ In which she sang.' In 'Asides on the Oboe' he asserts, 'The prologues are over. It is a question, now, /Of final belief. So, say that final belief must be in fiction.' And the stance of Nicholas Mosley quoted above, while much less extreme, does suggest that literature can perform some of the functions of religion in demonstrating to us the innate patterns in our own lives.

Science too can be used in a similar way. One rationale for its importance from the mid-seventeenth century onwards lies in its role as a replacement for the certainties provided by religion in the past. Indeed, it is scientific enquiry that has changed the very way we question the universe, the kind of answers we expect to the question 'why?'. Yet science provides us not with complete answers but with partial ones, not with certainties but with probabilities. It is one kind of knowledge, but it is *only* one kind of knowledge. And while some twentieth-century writers such as Durkheim have been optimistic about the 'rational society' that will, they believe, result from the direction a scientifically-based society is taking us, others see it as ushering in an era of cynicism and moral relativism. Max Weber prophesied 'mechanized petrification, embellished with a sort of convulsive self-importance'.[14]

If one wants to be optimistic, one can take heart from the fact that the scientific book that has attained the greatest popularity in the last decade is the one that promises most in the way of completeness, of meaning. Some have wondered at the immense sales of Stephen Hawking's *A Brief History of Time*, but, in the light of the argument in this chapter, at least one reason seems quite obvious. A history of time implicitly promises completeness, promises not just explanations but *an* explanation. It teases us into believing it will bring back the kind of wholeness that the great medieval theologies presented, but now with theology as a subsection of science rather than the other way around. Of course it cannot deliver all these things, and I am sure Stephen Hawking would insist he never claimed it could. Yet it ends with that most tantalizing and Faustian of desires – that we 'would know the mind of God'.[15]

At this point the deepest aims of religion and of science merge, and we meet ourselves again as at a medieval street corner hoping for explanations, for revelations, hoping above all to learn the truth about ourselves and the pattern of our own life which, somehow, we persist in believing must exist if only we could decipher it. 'A life should go toward something.'

2

CUSTOM AND CEREMONY

> *How but in custom and in ceremony*
> *Are innocence and beauty born?*
> W. B. Yeats, 'A Prayer for my Daughter'

If we accept that the desire for order and meaning is fundamental to most human beings, and that it has traditionally
been satisfied in this country chiefly by the Christian religion,
then we must examine what *kind* of religious experience, what
kind of worship, best fulfils this need today. The question is
the more pressing because of the diversity of types of worship
both within and outside the established Church, and because
of the rapidity and extent of change within the last two decades.

Is the custom and ceremony that still exists within much
of the life of the Church an anachronism? Does it exist even
in the Church primarily for the tourist trade? Little boys in
Eton collars singing masses written four hundred years ago,
inexplicable movements at the altar, incomprehensible words
in the prayers, the Church that Don Cupitt has described as
a 'museum'. Is it time we swept all this aside and made
religion simple, understandable, 'not mysterious', in the words
of a notable late-seventeenth-century deist? Surely this would
agree more closely with a society that above all seeks to
understand phenomena, to find rational explanations for
them, and has, to an amazing extent, succeeded in doing so.

It can be accomplished in at least two ways – either by
internalizing the truths of religion, recognizing they have no
objective truth but a necessary subjective relevance to our
own lives (a highly intellectual solution), or modernizing a
gospel message that is believed to be objectively true so that

its essentials are readily comprehensible to most people today (a popularist approach).

What both these solutions have in common is that they ignore or deny the importance of a continuing tradition of Christian worship, an historical continuum reaching back to the first century. If this tradition is at best decoration and at worst a barrier to the modern believer, as some would claim, then its disappearance is of little importance. But it is possible to argue that this is not the case, that, on the contrary, it is essential not only to Christian worship but to any religious belief that points to a life beyond this one. Thus Enoch Powell speculates,

> I'm prejudiced to the extent of supposing that whatever worshipping activity supplies requires a reference to the past. It may be that if man is an immortality-believing animal he is dependent upon the rehearsal and the assertion of his immortality – that the time dimension is crucial in anything which is satisfactory as a religious ritual. . . That it was so in the past is a necessary ingredient . . . 'as it was in the beginning is now and ever shall be. . .' with the assertion of a future because there was a past.

It is not just the need for the existence of *a* past that is at issue; it is a past bearing the signs and symbols of accumulated meaning. The philosopher C. Geertz asserts the need for sacred symbols, those things that are most profoundly meaningful despite, or even because of, their inability to be codified in wholly rational language.

> Sacred symbols function to synthesize a people's ethos – the tone, character, and quality of their life, its moral and aesthetic style and mood – and their world-view – the picture they have of the way things in sheer actuality are, their most comprehensive ideas of order. . .[1]

According to this view, religious ritual is not just a quaint survival from the past, a dim reflection of the reality we believe. It is rather that which convinces us of our belief. 'For it is in ritual – i.e. consecrated behaviour – that the conviction that religious conceptions are veridical and that religious directives are sound is somehow generated.'[2] Ritual is not merely a way of expressing our belief but is an instrument in its formation; it therefore is not accidental to the faith but essential.

The survey sought to discover the extent to which people today value and take advantage of the rituals the Church offers. It also attempted to measure how cognizant they are of the elements that go to make up liturgy and ritual and therefore how able they are to be likely to respond to them in a meaningful way.

The most common level at which the nominally Christian public meets church ritual is in the services of baptism, marriage, and burial. At this level, most people still want the Church to be there, performing its traditional role. Birth is seen as the least important of the three major steps in life for the Church to be involved in, though even here 59% claim 'it is important to hold a religious service'. This percentage rises to 76% for marriage and 82% for death. Differences between the three chief groups surveyed (students, teachers, and professionals) are not significant, though there were important differences, as one would expect, between Christians, agnostics, and atheists. However the percentage believing it important to hold a religious service for death was 53% even among atheists. The percentages among all Christian groups were very high, but here again Roman Catholics, at 97% scored 10% higher than Church of England adherents and 8% higher than Nonconformists, perhaps revealing the greater emphasis on the efficacy of sacraments in the Roman Catholic Church.

Whether all these people (particularly the agnostics and atheists) are happy with the kind of religious service the church offers on these occasions is, of course, another matter. A recent series of radio programmes on the BBC discussed the growing trend of people devising their own 'religious' services for these occasions. Such services have the advantage of being tailor-made for the individuals concerned – if, indeed, that is an advantage. For in becoming specific, they cease to be general; what they gain in particularity they lose in universality. And it is precisely at these moments of birth, marriage, and death that we are made most aware of our *common* humanity. 'Man that is born of a woman hath but a short time to live', rather than 'We remember John, whose life was tragically ended by an untimely car accident'. The latter statement may indeed reflect the feelings of those who knew John intimately, but its very specificity has removed it from ourselves and humanity in general. John's death becomes accidental in a sense other than that originally intended in the passage. It becomes a random, arbitrary event, robbed of meaning or significance for us. We are not John; we have not (yet at least) suffered an untimely accident.

One of the glories of the traditional liturgy is the way it avoids the severance of the particular and the general. We celebrate a particular marriage, but we also celebrate marriage as a whole. We mourn an individual we have loved, but we accept this death as part of a universal pattern of growth and decay – or more specifically of God's plan of birth, death, and regeneration for humanity. Again, it has the function of asserting order and through it meaning.

The *ad hoc* service raises other questions as well. It is not only cut off from traditional practice but from traditional language. For some this is one of its chief attractions, just as its particularity can also be seen as an attraction. Simple, direct statement says what it means and means what it says. 'I love you.' 'I will try to be faithful to you.' But there are problems with this approach. Firstly, it is based on a naive view of language that assumes words always mean the same thing to everyone. Yet to take the very obvious example above, it does not require much imagination to conjure up two marriage partners for whom the words 'love' and 'faithful' have quite different connotations. People are, admittedly, scarcely more likely to agree on what they are promising if they 'plight their troth' but in this case they may at least be led to explore what it is they are promising. Differences can be discussed, and easy assumptions critically examined. None of this is intended to prove that having people using incomprehensible language is a good thing, but given that the goal of complete comprehensibility in language is both naive and impossible, any argument based primarily on it is weak.

Beyond this is the question of what it is we wish language to do. Ideas about this have changed profoundly since the writing of the Book of Common Prayer and the King James translation of the Bible. In the Renaissance language was important not only to convey information and to argue but to persuade and to move. Treatises on rhetoric from the period link these different functions of language to different styles of speaking and writing – the plain style for argument, and the ornate for persuading and moving. The rhetorical devices of repetition, alliteration, simile, metaphor, parallel structure, and others whose names are now only the property of literary scholars were not intended primarily to convey information; they were designed to move us to repent our sins, to inspire us to lift our hearts up to God.

With the growing importance of science and industry, the fact-imparting role of language became more important, and the emotive function less so. The style of written English changed enormously in the second half of the seventeenth century, and has progressed further in roughly the same direction up to our own time. While present-day English is a more precise instrument for conveying scientific description and technical direction (and possibly for everyday communication) it is arguably less good for conveying the nuances of emotion and for literary expression.

What we expect of language has changed, and language has changed in conformity to those expectations. While it is now largely a utilitarian tool, in the sixteenth century it was one of the marks of personality, either noble or base. Indeed, it could be seen as a moral force for good or ill. Roger Ascham in *The Schoolmaster*, one of the first books on education written in English, makes just this claim:

> Ye know not what hurt ye do to learning, that care not for words but for matter, and so make a divorce betwixt the tongue and the heart. For . . . look upon the whole course of both the Greek and Latin tongue, and ye shall surely find that, when apt and good words began to be neglected . . . then also began ill deeds to spring.[3]

While few today would subscribe to the moral argument for words in the extreme form Ascham expresses it, the notion that language is not merely a conveyer of meaning but itself part of the meaning is still valid. David Martin reiterates this view when he says, 'If it really is the case that the *lex orandi* is the *lex credendi*, then as we alter the form of our prayer, we alter the substance of our faith.'[4] When modern churchgoers say they do not understand the language of the Prayer Book, they are not simply saying that they do not understand the words; they are saying (whether they know it or not) that they do not understand the way in which language was used at the time the Prayer Book was written.

This discrepancy between two differing ways of using language is at the heart of one aspect of the debate about the use of the ASB. I. R. Thompson in his article 'Gospel Message/Gospel Manifestation' deplores the language failure of the ASB as 'just one aspect of a profoundly religious and ultimately eschatological failure . . . a massive over-emphasis on the gospel as statement or message, and a corresponding very serious neglect of the gospel as *manifestation*.'[5]

A response to a use of language that seeks to move rather than simply to instruct or inform is not limited to those who understand the ancient theory behind it any more than a response to a Beethoven symphony is limited to those who can analyse it. On the contrary, David Martin claims that 'overhearing that prayerful syntax even the most casual passer-by, obsessed with the utilitarian and the pragmatic, can catch the hint of glory, even if he gives it no philosophic weight.'[6]

Martin might almost be giving a philosophical explanation of the experience described by Dell, the young girl in *Lives of Girls and Women* by Alice Munro, when she describes her reaction to her first encounter with the Anglican liturgy in this way:

> So here was what I had not known, but must always have suspected, existed, what all those Methodists and Congregationalists and Presbyterians had fearfully abolished – the theatrical in religion. From the very first I was strongly delighted. . . Ritual, which in other circumstances might have seemed wholly artificial, lifeless, had here a kind of last-ditch dignity.[7]

Against this is a whole school of thought in the Church (lumped together by the narrator in the passage above as 'Methodists, Congregationalists and Presbyterians', though by no means linked exclusively to those specific denominations) that distrusts seeing the liturgy as a vehicle for producing an emotional or dramatic effect. Margaret Drabble, raised as a Quaker, says she was 'brought up with a deep distrust of any ceremony, of any sort of theatrical religion'. Now when she goes into a Roman Catholic church she is 'shocked and delighted by the drama of the whole thing. . . But it's not *religion* to me. . .'

This response is not limited to those with a Nonconformist background. Although English drama began in the Church with the *quem quaeritus* plays which grew out of the liturgy, and although, as I have shown in chapter 1, the whole liturgy is highly dramatic in structure, there is an inherent distrust of 'drama' among many of the clergy and laity. Indeed, Michael Mayne, Dean of Westminster, suggested that one of the reasons people may not respond to religious services is 'partly because [they] do not have a proper sense of theatre. And I think that every act of worship is in one aspect an act of theatre.' He was the only clergyman of those I interviewed, however, to discuss a church service in this way at all.

At the heart of this reluctance seems to be a mistaken notion that the dramatic is not 'real', that what is well-produced is 'artificial', and therefore not 'sincere'. This seems to me to rest on naive notions of reality that confuse amateurism with sincerity and professionalism with artifice. Again, opposing this view, Michael Mayne says, 'It is a matter of presentation, a matter of actually communicating by doing something with enormous care'.

Beyond these questions of whether care in the 'performance' of the liturgy is appropriate, however, one has to ask to what extent people are still open to this experience of language – and to aesthetic experience in general. It is one thing to speak of the emotive element in language; it is another to assume that the same language (or music) produces a similar emotive effect on everyone. There are those who seem instinctively to respond to the 'great' in music or literature. The most remarkable example of this in my experience was a girl I knew at graduate school who told of first hearing on the radio, when she was a teenager, the opening chorus of the 'St Matthew Passion'. She had no previous knowledge of either the composer or the work, yet she immediately exclaimed, 'What is that!' recognizing, so she said, that here was something greater than any music she had ever heard before.

This kind of experience is by no means universal. The present Archbishop of Canterbury confesses to having been bored by church ceremony and music when he was a young man. Perhaps he was unfortunate in the kind of worship he encountered, but perhaps not. Indeed, some would deny that there is 'better' and 'worse' in church worship at all; it may be simply a matter of taste. The same literary critics who question the assignment of 'value' to works of literature would question the assumption that there is, in any absolute sense, 'better' and 'worse' in language, music, or liturgy. One of my academic colleagues stated as if it were the merest common-place: 'Value judgements (unless you believe in God) are entirely subjective'. The canon is 'out'. There is 'high' culture and 'popular' culture. One is not inherently preferable to the other. But her proviso, 'unless you believe in God', though intended as a throw-away putdown, should give the Church pause for thought. The implied corollary must be that if you *do* believe in God, then such judgements can have validity.

What few would deny is that, my exceptionally musical friend apart, our reactions are likely to be coloured by our experience; we respond to what we know. What the survey has shown is that this experience can no longer, even among the élite sample surveyed, be taken for granted. Familiarity with the works (both literary and musical) that have tradition-ally been regarded as classics in our society cannot be assumed. Custom and ceremony depend on a reliable trans-mission of historical knowledge and, even more important, an historical sense. The survey provides hard evidence that both are rapidly disappearing from present-day England.

First some bare statistics. Given a list of eleven prominent writers ranging chronologically from the sixteenth century to the present day, 23% of the sample were unable to name a single religious work by any writer. (The list comprised Bunyan, John Donne, T. S. Eliot, John Foxe, George Herbert, Gerard Manley Hopkins, C. S. Lewis, John Milton, John Henry Newman, Sir Thomas More, and Malcolm Mugger-idge – a fairly eclectic group including Catholics and Noncon-formists as well as Church of England.) John Bunyan was the only writer to whom more than half the group (59%) could attribute a work. Milton had to be content with 47% of whom most (37% of the total sample) could name *Paradise Lost*. C. S. Lewis, chiefly because of the popularity of his Narnia books, rated next in order of recognition, with T. S. Eliot

TABLE 3 *And for each one, are you familiar with anything of a religious nature he has written?* (col. %)

	SAMPLE GROUP				SEX		SUBJECTS				QUALIFICATIONS				POLITICS		SEES LIFE AS	
	Total	Stud-ents	Teach-ers	Profes-sionals	Male	Female	Scien-ces	Appl. Scien-ces	Arts	Vocat-ional	Post grad.	Degree	Dip-loma/ 'A' level	Other	Left	Right	Mean-ingful patt.	Chance series of events
Total	614	205	214	195	388	226	159	88	188	198	136	319	141	17	253	298	357	183
John Bunyan	59	28	79	70	59	59	50	53	63	70	80	49	63	59	62	57	66	46
John Donne	30	17	42	31	28	34	22	24	39	30	44	27	26	6	37	23	34	22
T. S. Eliot	34	21	46	34	32	37	23	22	44	39	49	29	32	24	42	26	38	27
John Foxe	8	3	12	9	9	7	6	3	12	8	13	6	8	6	10	6	8	7
George Herbert	15	11	23	12	15	16	8	14	24	13	26	15	7	6	21	12	18	11
Gerard Manley Hopkins	20	12	32	16	19	23	11	13	32	21	32	18	16	–	26	14	23	14
C. S. Lewis	44	29	61	40	39	51	39	28	53	46	60	40	39	24	52	36	50	33
John Milton	47	23	65	53	46	50	36	35	56	58	68	38	52	18	53	42	50	41
John Henry Newman	15	3	24	17	15	15	14	9	19	16	27	10	17	–	18	13	17	11
Sir Thomas More	25	16	33	27	26	24	16	22	34	27	40	21	23	18	31	21	25	23
Malcolm Muggeridge	21	5	30	28	23	18	18	18	22	24	38	13	21	29	23	20	25	17
None of these	23	45	9	15	25	20	29	32	18	17	10	29	22	24	18	27	18	32

		DENOMINATION				BELIEF			RELIGIOUS UPBRINGING		RELIGIOUS ATTENDANCE				SCHOOLING			
	Total	Cath-olic	C. of E.	Metho-dist	None	Chris-tian	Agno-stic	Athe-ist	Yes	No	Once week or more	Once month	Less often	Never	Non-den. state	Church-aff. state	Non-den. indep.	Church-aff. indep.
Total	614	60	350	76	94	385	142	78	332	281	161	87	192	174	371	70	93	79
John Bunyan	59	45	57	82	54	65	57	32	72	44	84	72	46	44	61	47	58	63
John Donne	30	30	30	21	36	29	37	21	34	25	41	32	26	22	28	31	30	37
T. S. Eliot	34	35	34	28	35	34	41	21	39	27	45	32	30	29	30	41	35	43
John Foxe	8	8	8	11	6	8	11	1	10	6	12	11	6	5	6	7	9	19
George Herbert	15	18	15	16	13	15	20	9	17	13	25	18	9	11	12	16	16	29
Gerard Manley Hopkins	20	32	19	22	18	21	25	12	26	14	32	22	15	15	15	27	27	30
C. S. Lewis	44	55	40	47	40	48	40	31	52	34	70	46	32	32	39	56	43	57
John Milton	47	55	47	42	43	50	52	27	56	37	66	51	42	34	44	54	54	49
John Henry Newman	15	30	14	17	9	17	15	5	20	9	30	15	10	6	11	21	16	29
Sir Thomas More	25	53	23	20	26	24	32	21	31	19	35	25	19	24	20	43	24	35
Malcolm Muggeridge	21	38	20	14	18	23	23	12	27	15	32	22	14	18	20	31	16	23
None of these	23	15	26	12	27	17	26	44	14	34	6	15	30	34	22	21	27	23

trailing well behind with only 34% of those surveyed able to name anything he had written, and some of these cited 'the cat poems'. After this it is downhill all the way with poor John Foxe, whose *Book of Martyrs* was once compulsory reading on every good Protestant's Sunday afternoon, coming in last at 8%.

The true picture is even more depressing than the figures alone reveal. In every sample of those who *claimed* they knew a work by these writers, a significant portion, ranging from 3% to 7%, ended up saying they 'did not know' or 'couldn't remember' its name. Also, there were a reasonable number of misattributions. Indeed, I conclude that certain well-known works of English literature are 'free floating' in the public consciousness, ready to be attributed to any likely author presented. *The Mill on the Floss* and Gray's 'Elegy' are two such works that kept surfacing although, of course, neither George Eliot nor Thomas Gray was among the writers on the list. And what of the individual who, pressed to name a religious work by Milton, responded ' "A" level work', or another who came up with 'something with "devil"?'

In assessing these results, it must be emphasized again that the sample was *not* a portion of the population at large. Nearly all those surveyed either have or are currently working for a university degree. Many have postgraduate training. One third of the sample are school teachers. What these people do not know now is unlikely to be transmitted to future generations. University students, as in all the knowledge questions, score particularly badly with a stunning 45% unable to name a single work by any of the authors.

Even more depressing in relation to this particular study is the fact that such knowledge as exists does not appear to be linked in any direct way to religious commitment. Indeed, in most cases agnostics did significantly better at naming works than Christians (though atheists, possibly because a high proportion of them were also first-year university students, did particularly badly). Only Bunyan and C. S. Lewis were more likely to be known by Christians than agnostics, and in the case of Donne, Eliot, Herbert, and More, the agnostics did very much better.

Where religious affiliation does seem to make a difference is in the *kind* of religious writers one is familiar with. Thus only 45% of Catholics can name a work by Bunyan as against 82% of Nonconformists, but when one comes to Hopkins, Newman, and More the roles are reversed, with significantly more Roman Catholics than Nonconformists able to name works. Also, if one looks at figures for church attendance, rather than self-assessment as 'Christian', 'agnostic', or 'atheist', then there is a positive correlation in all cases with knowledge of these writers.

One other important factor is education. With the exception of three authors, those respondents educated in church-affiliated independent schools scored higher than those educated either in church-affiliated state schools or in non-denominational schools, either independent or state. In two of the three exceptions (Sir Thomas More and Malcolm Muggeridge), however, it was the church-affiliated state schools that topped the list – not the non-denominational independent schools as one might have expected if this were primarily a matter of state versus independent education.

Overall, general intellectual ability seems to be the most significant variable here. A separation of the responses of students into three groups (Cambridge, Liverpool/Bristol/Sheffield universities, and Leicester/Newcastle/Kingston polytechnics) produced a statistical result of almost unbelievably neat proportions. Of those at Cambridge 31% were unable to name a single work by any author; at the other three universities (combined) it was 44%, and at the three polytechnics (again combined) it was 57% – a 13% increase for each group.

The broad statistics for music appear at first to be more encouraging than for literature, but this is probably only because two popular composers (Andrew Lloyd Webber and Cliff Richard) were included, thereby throwing the net wider so that only 15% failed to name any religious work by any composer. However, one can scarcely be encouraged by results that show only 46% can name anything by Bach, and a mere 30% anything by Britten. Tallis, Vaughan Williams, Byrd, and Stanford are all relatively unknown with less than 20% able to name anything they have written. Indeed, a principal wind player in one of the country's major symphony orchestras was unable to name anything by Tallis or Byrd, which shows how specialized and compartmentalized our knowledge has become. These two composers are not part of the orchestral repertoire and hence not known by an orchestral player.

Unlike the literature, there is a positive correlation in nearly all cases between being a 'Christian' and knowledge of these religious composers, and a similar correlation with church attendance. The most significant differences, however, have little to do with religious adherence at all but with whether the respondents had sung with a choir, apart from a school choir. (Oddly enough, playing a musical instrument, while correlating overall positively, did not produce anything like the same degree of difference, and while type of general education appeared to influence the results much as it did in the literature, its effect here was not nearly as pronounced.) One would conclude, therefore, that general musical education is a more important influence on whether one knows religious music than experience of church worship. Although, having said that, it is possible that a fair proportion of those who sang with a choir did so with a church choir, in which case the two groups (musical and religiously committed) would overlap and reinforce one another. In general, however, one has to conclude that the Church is not a particularly important vehicle for passing on a knowledge of religious writing or music.

It is possible to argue that these things do not matter. Margaret Drabble questions, 'Why should they have knowledge of these things? These things belong to the past; they belong to the future. I don't feel this sense of the importance of the past. I sometimes think the past is a dead hand, and that if we knew less about it we'd be able to cope better with where we're going to.' Yet later in the same interview she speaks of her own experience singing hymns within the otherwise austere Quaker worship and concludes, 'I find the singing of hymns so moving still. . . They are a link with one's entire childhood, one's past, with the continuity of certain events. . . And as they're being sung it's as though there were a single thread through life.' It would seem that while knowledge of the past may be rejected as unimportant at an intellectual level, it continues (for those who possess it) to have value at an emotional one.

In addition to a knowledge of religious literature and music in general, the survey sought to discover the extent of people's familiarity with the Bible and the liturgy of the Church. This was done in two ways. They were asked to quote from memory, if possible, a Bible passage and a passage from the liturgy (in both cases, other than the Lord's Prayer). They were also given a number of quotations from the liturgy and the Bible to identify. The results from both parts of this question were pretty deplorable.

Overall only 50% of those interviewed knew *any* Bible passage from memory, and that percentage rose only to 59% even among those who claimed to be Christian. Among those who attended church once a week or more the figure was still only 76%. Teachers, as an occupational group, did particularly well (67%), and arts graduates did somewhat better than those trained in the sciences. The most significant difference, however, was between the students and any other group. Only 27% of students claim to know any Bible passage other than the Lord's Prayer from memory. (And it would have been a brave interviewer who would have dared to discover how many knew even the Lord's Prayer by heart.) It should also be recorded that most of the responses from all groups were from a very limited range of passages. Once one eliminated the opening verse of Psalm 23 and the beginning of Genesis or St John's Gospel, there was little left. The response of one student wit just about summed up the situation: 'Jesus wept'.

The answers to a similar question about the liturgy were predictably worse. Only 39% of the total sample claimed to know anything from memory, 48% of Christians, and 70% of those who attended church once a week or more. Roman Catholics appear, on the face of it, to have done astonishingly better than any other denomination (77% against 38% for Church of England and 34% for Nonconformists). It has to be recorded, however, that the quantity of 'Hail Mary's' was overwhelming! Students educated in church-affiliated state schools did significantly better here (66% positive response) than those in any other type of school, including church-affiliated independent schools, whose positive response rate was only 46%. Both here and in the question on Bible passages, there is a high degree of positive correlation with religious upbringing at home.

Not only could surprisingly few people attempt to quote

any passages from the Bible or liturgy but, in most cases when they did so, they were astonishingly inaccurate. Can this also be attributed to a belief that only the meaning, the 'gist' of the thing matters, that the actual words, the phrases, the rhythms, are unimportant?

Learning by heart plays a much less important role in education than it did even thirty years ago, and that may in part explain the failure of nearly three-quarters of the students to quote anything at all from the Bible or liturgy. But there is another factor as well that particularly affects the younger generation, and that is the modern proliferation of translations of the Bible and versions of the liturgy. In follow-up interviews, the variety of translations was often cited as a reason for the inability to know anything by heart. Further corroboration of this view comes from the fact that of those who could quote a passage from the Bible, 50% did so from the Authorized Version (King James or, for Roman Catholics, Douai). Other responses were divided among numerous modern translations, with none named by as many as 10% of the respondents. 'Don't knows' accounted for 20% and, assuming they divided in roughly the same proportion as those who claimed to know, the actual number of those quoting the Authorized Version is considerably higher than 50%. Only among students was the number citing the Authorized Version equalled by those citing a modern translation, the New International Version (14% each). Of the small proportion of those able to offer a quotation at all, 43% did not know which translation they were quoting.

Similarly, most of those who could quote part of the liturgy or a prayer (and knew which version they were quoting) did so from the 1662 Prayer Book. Again, students were the sole exception, with slightly more (17% against 15%) quoting from a modern language version. (Roman Catholics are, naturally, an exception here since the only liturgy in English they possess is modern language.) As with the Bible passages, a surprising number (37% overall, 69% of students), had no idea which version they were quoting – again reinforcing the view that they simply are unaware of language as worthy of attention in itself.

Three general conclusions follow from these results. The coming generation is (1) much less likely to know the Bible and liturgy than its predecessors; (2) where passages are known from memory they are likely to be from traditional, not modern translations; and (3) there is little concern with language among either the older or the younger generation. Further, those young people who, exceptionally, know some Bible passages from memory are likely to be Evangelical; this surely is the explanation for the popularity of the New International Version among this group.

All of this begs the question as to whether knowing these things by memory is of any value or importance. First, does it indicate anything about the state of the Church and faith? There are those, among them Bishop Vincent Nichols as well as a substantial number of Church of England clergy, who would say it does not. Bishop Nichols jokingly pointed out that he usually was not that far from a Bible when he wanted to look something up, so why go to the trouble of memorizing it? This ties in with the modern educational theory that argues that education is not about learning facts but about learning how to discover and apply information.

The Bible, however, has never been used in the past chiefly as an encyclopedia or source book. 'Thy word shall be a lamp unto my feet and a light unto my path.' It is a text that must be internalized, constantly present, if it is to be of value. And there may be times in life when one is *not* as able to read a Bible as one might wish. Characterizing the lack of learning by heart as 'very bad', Lord Runcie continued, 'Anybody who is a good pastor . . . will know that some of the most impressive deaths are of people who are able to mutter "Into your hands O Lord" and things like that, simple things.' And the Dean of Westminster, while rating memorization overall as 'useful, not essential' added drily, that it 'may be rather useful when you're dying'.

If we are to reject the need for the traditional familiarity with the Bible, we must be aware that we are rejecting a whole dimension of religious experience and awareness. The notion of the word of God as a guide and protection throughout life's journey has largely disappeared. What one 'understands' on Sunday but cannot recall with any accuracy on Monday is unlikely to be a dominant force in one's life. Paradoxically, it would seem that the multiplicity of translations that were designed to make the Bible 'understandable' and accessible to all have resulted in its being 'known' in any depth by fewer people.

It might be argued that while people do not carry the words of Scripture as a constant part of their intellectual baggage as they once did, nevertheless, they do recognize and recall it (and its meaning) when it is presented to them. A second part of this section of the survey belies even this limited optimism. Here those interviewed were given a series of phrases from the Bible and the liturgy and were asked to identify them as closely as possible. 50% were able to place 'The Lord is my shepherd' as coming from Psalm 23, and 57% knew that 'And there were shephereds, abiding in the fields' came from the Christmas story in the Bible (though only 26% knew it was from St Luke's Gospel), but after that there was little that was encouraging. More people (33%) identified 'In the beginning was the Word', as coming from Genesis than (correctly) as the opening of St John's Gospel (30%). Only 36% knew that 'Blessed are the meek, for they shall inherit the earth', was one of the Beatitudes, though a further 7% identified it as coming from St Matthew's Gospel. This particular question also produced one of the most wonderful 'howlers' of the study. Under 'other' one respondent carefully filled in 'Platitudes'. Nothing in the rest of his/her replies would indicate that this was an attempt at wit!

Once one moved from the Bible into the liturgy, the results were even more depressing – although it must be acknowledged that in some of these questions, those who were not Church of England were at a distinct disadvantage. Only 19% (23% of C. of E.) recognized that 'Almighty God, our heavenly father, we have sinned against you and our fellow men' came from the confession in the ASB Eucharist, and even fewer (11% overall, 14% C. of E.) identified the opening of the Matins and Evensong confession from the 1662 Prayer Book ('Almighty and most merciful Father; we have erred, and strayed from thy ways like lost sheep'). In each case some respondents (14% and 15% respectively) identified the passage simply as a 'confession'. The use of similar passages from both ASB and Book of Common Prayer was, of course, deliberate. The results, which favour the ASB, would seem to show that there is no turning back; what is no longer widely in use has been lost; but the new, as yet, has not become universally known and accepted.

Matins seems to be in decline. Only 10% overall (13% of Anglicans) could identity the opening phrase of the *Te Deum*. As for occasional services, 45% were unable to identify at all 'Man that is born of a woman hath but a short time to live,' and only 33% identified it with any precision. The giving of the candle to the child in baptism ('This is to show that you have passed from darkness to light') was correctly identified in a general way by only 29%, with Roman Catholics here doing slightly better than Church of England (36% and 32%). Given that the total sample excluded all people who were adherents of non-Christian faiths, these results can scarcely be cause for complacency.

In the last question in this section of the questionnaire, those interviewed were presented with four postcards and asked to describe the subject; all were of religious paintings hanging in the National Gallery. The *Adoration of the Kings* was relatively easy, with only 10% failing to respond in a generally correct way. But with the *Betrayal in the Garden* the percentage of 'don't knows' and 'other' rose to 20%, and for the *Annunciation* it was 28%. The *Martyrdom of St Sebastian* was identified correctly by only 12%. An amazing 57% thought it was a picture of the Crucifixion – in some instances qualifying this identification by saying it was a 'poor' picture!

The objection that can be raised to all the foregoing is that it confuses knowledge with faith, that it treats religion like an examination; man (or woman) will be saved not by works or by faith alone, nor even by every word that proceeds from the mouth of God, but by the quantity of words of Scripture and liturgy that he or she can spew out at a passing interviewer from Gallup. Thus caricatured, it is easy to dismiss the results of the survey as unimportant or not dealing with essentials. But the caricature of the opposite position – that faith exists unsupported by any knowledge of its content, that hope survives devoid of substance – is just as absurd. Even the notion that there is a knowledge that somehow exists without any visible evidence or ability to recall it seems unconvincing. I have argued for a distinction between what is merely known intellectually, and what has been absorbed deeply and subliminally into the whole consciousness of a person's life. The difficulty is that it would seem the former must precede the latter; what has never been on the surface cannot be internalized, and I have problems with a notion of concepts that have been so deeply internalized they are no longer accessible to memory.

The only exception to this argument would seem to be that of intuitive knowledge, the province of seers and saints. These have never been known to appear in sufficient quantity to affect the statistical results of any study. However, this belief in instinctive knowledge and faith may well be one of the factors underlying the popularity of some modern Evangelical sects that promote just such a notion of Christianity.

While the implications of these results for the state of the faith as such can, I recognize, be disputed, those for the traditional Christian culture of England seem beyond debate. What was known is known no longer; the words, the phrases of music that were common to at least the strata of society the survey covered, are rapidly disappearing. The very static of the mind, those words and phrases that make their way without any conscious effort over and over in our thoughts when we are not deliberately occupied with some intellectual task, has changed. What the 'new static' is, and what effect such a profound shift in our mental processes will have in general on our society, is the province of psychologists and sociologists. One fears it must be impoverishing.

In *A Portrait of the Artist as a Young Man*, Cranly says to Stephen Daedelus, 'Your mind is supersaturated with the religion in which you say you disbelieve'. Today it seems we may have passed even that watershed. Our minds are supersaturated with no such thing though, by a curious irony, it is those who disbelieve who are most likely to be among those few still 'supersaturated'.

My elder son, reading music at university, after making a pilgrimage to watch the sun rise over a deserted beach, confessed: 'I was so annoyed; when the sun came up all I could think of was that wretched McDonald's "day in the life of" ad.' I suppose it might have been the magnificent morning hymn 'Father we praise thee, now the night is over', set to a Rouen church melody, with its multiple associations linking the literal morning with the final radiant morning of the second coming. But what is gone from the all-pervasive subconsciousness is gone. It cannot always be conjured up at will.

Advertisements have come not only to replace music and poetry in the subconscious but to act as one of the major forces that dissociate words and music from their context. Watching (inadvertently) an advertisement for Ford cars on television, I was jolted to full consciousness by the background music, which was unmistakably Verdi's *Dies Irae*. As the cars rolled on and off the screen to this stirring tune I pondered the message. 'Going to hell in a Ford?' With some persistence I tracked down the people who created this particular advertisement. No, they did not know the medieval poem; no, they had no idea what it was about, and, anyway, the version of the music they had used was a pop one with no words. Why had they chosen it? Chiefly rhythm. So no irony was intended? 'There's no time for irony in an ad', came back the reply. And this is only one particular example. 'Wachet auf' sells Lloyds Bank, Tallis' 'Forty Part Motet' pushes Harrods' china sales.

Crossing the boundaries between the secular and the sacred is not new, as witness Christopher Tye's 'Western Wind Mass' and many other examples from the Middle Ages and Renaissance. The sanctification of the secular has good theological precedent and justification. But this existed within a society that did not perceive the boundaries as we do; all was potentially sacred. What we see now is not the union of sacred and secular but an ignorance of context, a lack of awareness or caring peculiar to our modern society.

How have we come to lose words, music, a sense of ceremony – things which, the survey indicates, at a deep level sustain the order and meaning that we most desire? First, there are the easy answers – the education system, which takes more than its share of blame these days for whatever is wrong in society. We have already noted the connection between general educational theory and the loss of knowing things from memory. More specifically, the state schools have largely ceased to give Christian instruction for a host of reasons connected with the change from a relatively homogeneous to a pluralistic society. Children who do not become familiar with the Bible, prayers and hymns through church attendance are unlikely to do so at school, though the survey has shown that church state schools have been more successful at passing on this knowledge than even church-affiliated independent schools, while the latter produce students who are more generally knowledgeable about works of religious literature, art, and music.

The modern home has different but no less significant problems in acting as an adequate transmitter of religious faith and knowledge. In my own home, from the time I was quite young, we read and discussed a passage from the Bible every Sunday evening. When the Revised Standard Version of the New Testament was published we frequently read the same passage in both translations and talked about the differences between them. I could therefore claim that not only my first knowledge of the Bible but my first rudimentary experience of comparing texts and translations came from within my immediate family. And this, I should add, was a working-class family with no scholarly pretensions whatsoever.

It is the family, not the Church, to which Yeats is referring in the passage that prefaces this chapter, conjuring up a whole traditional way of life centred on family, inheritance, and tradition that has virtually disappeared. The question that he could pose merely rhetorically is now a real one. Not only does the family not usually take on this role, but the family itself is ceasing to exist at an alarming rate. A modern single parent struggling to keep his or her children fed, clothed, and housed, is unlikely to have the time, energy, or inclination to pass on a religious heritage – or any other sort, for that matter. Cut off from the past themselves, living in isolation in an urban setting, such parents are more likely to give priority to getting good grades in school and to 'looking out for yourself', than to passing on something they themselves never experienced or only dimly remember. Thus at the outset the child is programmed towards those individual goals of self-fulfilment and enjoyment of life that we found to be dominant in the first chapter. 'Innocence and beauty' may well appear to be irrelevant or even counter-productive qualities in the kind of world they see their children encountering.

Yet it is the religious influence, or lack of it, in the family that the survey reveals to be most crucial for an individual's future development. Of those who claim to attend church once a week or more, 78% say they were 'brought up religiously at home'. Of those who 'never' attend church, only 33% were brought up religiously. The home also affects the choice of schooling, which in turn reinforces the religious or secular ethos of the home. Of those who attended a church-affiliated state school 71% claimed to have been brought up religiously, while only 51% of those attending either non-denominational state or independent schools were.[8]

Just as culpable as the schools and the home, however, is the Church itself by making, as I have argued earlier in this chapter, a division between tradition and conviction, the ceremonial and the sincere. There is the historical sense, the continuity with the past, ossified and artificial, and there is 'real' worship taking place in the here and now, unmediated by anything that has gone before. It has to be admitted that some churchgoers do give ammunition to this point of view.

A retired gentleman whom I met recently at a christening party was quite candid about the reasons for which he supported his local, rural church. He claimed no particular faith or conviction, but he felt strongly that the existence of this little church, with its irregular services of Matins, which he did attend, and its even more infrequent Eucharists, which by and large he did *not* attend, was important for reasons of continuity. Maybe he did not value the teaching of the Church as he should, he admitted, but it ought to be there for future generations who might judge things differently. It must survive and he, by acting as churchwarden, was trying to ensure it did. Naturally, he was opposed to modern language services, and naturally he disapproved of much the new vicar did, but he would continue to support his local church with both his time and money.

This, I could not help reflecting, was a living caricature of the person the modern Church most despises, though he would have been in very good standing in the eighteenth century. Here the divorce between tradition and faith is extreme and explicit. And there are other examples, one of which was described to me by the former Archbishop of Canterbury. Despite asserting, 'History and tradition are important to me; they influence my faith more than metaphysics', Lord Runcie admitted that he found the congregation at the Westminster Abbey service commemorating Cranmer in many ways disappointing. While there were obviously genuine lovers of the Prayer Book present, 'there were also the sort of literary thugs who are keener on the Prayer Book for keeping the lower orders in place than for elevating the spirit. I felt there were an uncomfortable number of them around.'

But need this divorce between the external forms and the true faith be thus extreme? As long as the Church assumes that it must, then it will consciously or unconsciously assist in this divorce. What has been lost, and is being lost, in the process is the subject of the next chapter.

3

CHRISTIANITY *OR* CULTURE

Why put them off with all the cultural baggage? It sets up a resistance.
They're bored before you even get into all that stuff.
David Hare, *Racing Demon*

I think . . . music . . . art . . . buildings . . . don't contain God, that
would be impossible, but they enable us to draw near to God, and God
to draw near to us.
Lord Runcie, former Archbishop of Canterbury

You are considerably more likely to believe that maintaining
historic buildings is an important role of the Church if you
are an agnostic or an atheist than if you are a Christian. This
was one of the more bizarre (though not entirely surprising)
results of the survey. Behind this rather amusing statistical
fact, however, lies a little-discussed aspect of the Church in
England today. It is both perceived to be, and in large
measure is, opposed to anything that can be seen as 'intellectual', 'esoteric', 'élitist'. The church that once preserved most
of what survived of western civilization in remote corners of
the country like Iona, now seems concerned to disburden itself
of its cultural trappings as fast as possible. The union that
T. S. Eliot envisaged between Christianity, culture, and
society in general ('Christianity *and* Culture') is now unthink-
able. Indeed, the very basis of this study may be suspect in
the eyes of the Church because it begins from an assumption
that the relationship between the Church and our society's
culture (understood as traditional, 'high' culture) is a matter
of importance, and that the Church has a role to play in this
area. It is an assumption that is questioned by those outside
the Church as well.

Imaginative literature seems to clarify the situation in a

way that nothing else has done, or has dared to do. Penelope Lively's novel, *Judgement Day* sets out the problem in a fairly extreme, exaggerated form. In its opening scene, Clare Paling, an agnostic and art connoisseur, is looking at the doom painting in the local church of the village to which she and her family have just moved. Here she is found by the vicar, one George Radwell, who knows nothing about doom paintings (the devils remind him of the 'red devil' aerial acrobats) but assumes that, because Clare is in his church and looking at something, she must be Church of England. Her biting comment brings him up short: ' "Interest in ecclesiastical architecture", said Mrs Paling sweetly, "is not restricted to Christians. And infrequent amongst them, I've noticed." '[1]

Here the oppositions, the lines of demarcation, are very clear. It is not just that the vicar cannot conceive of anyone being interested in church wall paintings who is not a committed Christian, but that Clare assumes that no one who *is* a practising Christian would be very likely to be.

It comes as no surprise when Clare, who eventually does go into the church for a service of worship, rather than just treating it as a museum/art gallery, takes the hapless vicar to task once more for the modern language versions of Psalm 23 and 1 Corinthians 13. Her reaction ('What have they done, these people? Where is the majesty of language? Words were a matter for martyrdom, time was. Have they exchanged a birthright for this mess of pottage?') reflects back on the discussion of liturgy in the previous chapter. The vicar's defence is straightforward and predictably unoriginal: ' "It's all made more meaningful, putting things in a straightforward, modern style." ' He adds, almost plaintively, ' "It's only words, after all." '

> 'Only words? *Only* words! Oh, dear. But you see, words are what I do believe in. They're all we've got.' . . .
>
> 'And there are you people,' she went on, 'chucking out some of the finest words in the language. If you aren't to be trusted with that what are you to be trusted with?' (p. 83).

In the end the novel overstates its case; George Radwell, the vicar who entered the Church because of a typing error, is just a bit *too* stupid, too bumblingly well-meaning, to escape being a caricature. But the battle lines drawn in the passage quoted above, even if exaggerated, ring true. They are reflected in letters to *The Times* by writers and musicians who claim that the church is destroying its cultural heritage, which are then replied to by clergy who claim that (a) that is not necessarily the case, (b) even if it is it doesn't matter because such things are not the chief concern of the Church and (c) the people complaining never come near a service of worship anyway. What is sad about these arguments, both fictional and real, is the exclusiveness of the opposing positions. Clare believes *only* in words; 'They're all we've got'. The vicar knows nothing about words and cares less. 'It's *only* words.' The *double entendre* on the use of 'only' (solely and merely) makes explicit the chasm separating their understanding and beliefs.

This is particularly ironic in the light of the traditional connections between the 'word' (of writing, sermons, poetry) and the Word, the divine Logos. It is impossible to understand theories of seventeenth-century preaching, or even the (to us) astonishing seriousness with which people like Donne and Herbert took that preaching, without understanding this connection between the word spoken and written and its incarnation in Christ:

> The Son of God is . . . the word; God made us with his word, and with our words we make God so farre, as that we make up the mysticall body of Christ Jesus with our prayers, with our whole liturgie, and we make the naturall body of Christ appliable to our soules, by the words of Consecration in the sacrament, and our soules apprehensive, and capable of that body, by the word Preached.[2]

Today the word spoken or preached has been reduced to an arbitrary symbol of communication, and the Logos is a frayed Greek idea, assumed (naturally) to be incomprehensible to anyone outside a theological college – and to most within one. The word has become mundane, and the Word obscure; the importance of both has, significantly, disappeared together.

If the Church is distrustful of 'culture', it has to be admitted that literary culture at least has been giving the Church a pretty bad press for hundreds of years. Even Shakespeare's clergy are at best incompetents (Friar Lawrence) or pompous asses, their very language reflecting a pretentiousness their real intellectual ability cannot sustain.

> A contract of eternal bond of love,
> Confirmed by mutual joinder of your hands,
> Attested by the holy close of lips,
> Strengthened by interchangement of your rings,
> And all the ceremony of this compact
> Sealed in my function, by my testimony
> Since when, my watch hath told me, toward my grave
> I have travelled but two hours.
>
> (Twelfth Night, V.i.159–66)

At worst they are charlatans: 'And I would I were the first that ever dissembled in such a gown'. The clergy of Jane Austen and Trollope hardly redeem the picture, and looking at a selection of novels and plays written in the last decade, expectations do not seem to have risen.

Indeed, if one is to take these literary models as one's yardstick, there is some evidence that words and meaning, beauty and faith, culture and Christianity have become generally divorced from one another in our society. In the novel *Incline our Hearts* by A. N. Wilson the narrator, Julian Ramsay, grows up in a vicarage family, steeped in the externals of church ritual and liturgy. He observes, however, that in his uncle's mind these things are inexplicably linked to an obsession with a family of the minor nobility; they seem to have little practical bearing on 'real' life. Here the link I have sought to establish between order, ceremony, and meaning in the preceding chapters breaks down. Ritual appears to give shape only, not meaning, to life. Indeed, the whole book is an admirable example of the survival of the shell of religion without the substance, the intellectual knowledge without the conviction.

Even more depressing is the portrait of clerical life in Susan Howatch's recent novel, *Scandalous Risks*. Here Venetia, a wealthy, titled young lady of no particular occupation, takes up residence in the close of Salisbury Cathedral and falls in love with the dean, Aysgarth, who more than reciprocates her passion.

Venetia's father sounds like a more extreme version of my churchwarden acquaintance.

> 'In his opinion all loyal English people ought to go through the initiation rites of the Church of England – it's part of our tribal heritage, like learning about King Alfred burning the cakes and memorising the patriotic speeches from *Henry V* and singing "Land of Hope and Glory" at the last night of the Proms.'[3]

Venetia is in many ways her father's daughter, and her own reaction to the cathedral evensong (after which she frequently has her trysts with the dean) displays just that divorce of cultural and aesthetic experience from 'religion' that has made the Church so distrustful of its own heritage.

> I liked the weekday choral evensong. It required no effort apart from kneeling down and standing up at regular intervals, and there was no sermon either to stretch the brain or induce rigor mortis. The choirboys sang in their unearthly voices; the vicars-choral bayed with authority; the vergers marched around providing touches of ceremonial; the clergy lolled meditatively in their stalls. I thought it was all so luxuriously restful, like a hot bath garnished with an expensive perfume, and as I watched the sun slant through the great west window I thought how clever God was to have invented the Church of England, that national monument dedicated to purveying religion in such an exquisitely civilised form. (p. 84)

This is the *reductio ad absurdum* of those attitudes among 'intellectuals' and 'aesthetes' that the Church (rightly) despises. It is also the extreme illustration of the title of this chapter. Sitting in the most exquisite cathedral in the country, listening to some of the finest music, Venetia can relate this only to entirely personal and hedonistic experiences.

Although published in 1991, the novel is set in the sixties in the period just after the publication of John Robinson's *Honest to God*. This work, with its emphasis on 'love' as the ground of all religious feeling, provides much of the theological justification for the action. But tied to the particular affair between Venetia and the dean, Robinson's 'love' begins to sound very much like special pleading, and Howatch provides an antidote in the form of a reply to *Honest to God* being written by the fictitious Bishop of Salisbury.

> Christianity is indeed about love but it is also about salvation and redemption. It is directed not towards a so-called modern man who lives some idyllic existence in which every problem can be solved with a kiss and a cuddle. It deals with people as they are – and very often they're suffering, floundering amidst tragedy. . . What has Dr Robinson to say to these people? Absolutely nothing. You must say rather more than: 'All you need is love!' to someone who is tortured by guilt, racked with grief or overpowered by despair. When a man is being crucified during his personal Good Friday, he needs someone who symbolises Easter Sunday and the redemptive love of Christ, not some sunny-natured fool who bounces around at the foot of the cross and showers him with sentimental good will. (p. 422)

The conventional conflict between bishop and dean adds human interest to this theological debate. In the end, however, the bishop and his wife emerge as schemers, puppeteers, and the dean as a self-deceiving charlatan. One is left with the impression that the author has grasped the essential issues and accurately observed the surfaces, but has not entered the life described in any real imaginative depth.

The work that purports to deal most exclusively and comprehensively with the Church in this decade is David Hare's *Racing Demon* which played successfully for a long run at the National. This play should cause the Church some disquiet both because of the six clergy and bishops in the play not one emerges remotely as a positive ideal and, even worse, from comments he has made about the play it appears that David Hare himself believes he has provided one.

Racing Demon covers everything. There is the bishop who believes in liturgy and ritual but can give no good reason for this beyond the fact that it is 'the one thing that unites us', though anyone who has read thus far in this book might just as easily conclude it is one of the chief things that divides us. He tells Lionel, the team rector, that his one duty is to 'put on a show'. Lionel is unconvinced. He is the stereotype clerical social worker, always helping people in a rather wishy-washy way, while neglecting his wife and hopelessly alienating his children. His three assistants are all well-meaning disasters of different types. 'Streaky' Bacon is good-hearted but essentially looks out for himself and his own welfare; he is happiest when drunk or maudlin. Harry is a tortured homosexual (obligatory in modern religious plays or novels), eventually exposed by the Sunday papers. And finally there is Tony, who is not just benignly ineffective like the others but positively dangerous, a rampant Evangelical, rushing into the lives of people he doesn't understand, and quite as narrow (though different) in his approach as the bishop: 'It's numbers, you see. That's what it is, finally. You have to get them in. Once they're there, you can do anything.'[4] Kingston, the suffragan bishop, parodies the Church's desire for compromise, pleasing all, offending none.

Everything in this play is set up only to be undercut. Lionel, who believes he has 'friends' and who *be*friends everyone, discovers when his wife is ill that he doesn't 'know a soul'. He talks a great deal about the failure of the Church to connect 'with ordinary people's lives'. Its job is 'mainly to listen and to learn. From ordinary, working people' (p. 3). But there is a suspicion that his ready identification with these people springs in some part from his own sense of failure. It is charged that he is 'tired' because he gets no strength from the gospel. 'He reeks of personal failure. And anguish. Like so much of the church' (p. 49).

Against this, Tony, the Evangelical, believes in an interventionist approach. One does not only listen to problems, one 'fixes' them. His intervention, however, ends in violence, with the person he seeks to help substantially worse off than before, cleaning the floors of a church that cannot afford to pay her a decent wage. He excuses his failure by insisting that these things ('social work') are not what really matters: 'Christ didn't come to do social work. He came to preach repentance' (p. 20). Yet there is a curious confusion in his own thinking between this 'salvationist' stance and the desire for success and numbers described above. It is this obsession with success that really cuts him off from Lionel and makes him the natural ally of the bishop. Both want the Church to be 'successful', and each claims spiritual validity for the widely different methods by which he seeks to achieve this.

The Bishop of Kingston, the practical politician, talks of the tensions 'of the job', the difficulty of holding Church and state together 'by a single thread', which he then shouts is only 'dental floss' (p. 42).

Naturally, Lionel is against traditional liturgy – possibly any liturgy at all – for reasons that sound distressingly familiar. 'The moment you start using all the language, you distance people. And it's not important [the language]. He's there. He loves people whether they know it or not. Why put them off with all the cultural baggage? It sets up a resistance. They're bored before you even get into all that stuff' (p. 59). Lionel seems to assume the people you are dealing with are outside the mainstream of traditional cultural life, and therefore the 'baggage' is totally foreign to them. What is more, based on the results of the current survey, he is absolutely right!

Racing Demon demonstrates the love/hate relationship with the Church that is so familiar among writers. The problem with the play is that while it gives a brilliant and amusing picture of the surface, it, like *Scandalous Risks*, never seems to penetrate beneath this surface. The characters remain caricatures; the plot an ingenious device for displaying as many of the extreme positions of the present-day Church as possible. One could not say that the portrait was entirely false; but it never seems entirely real or true either. David Hare seems to have more sympathy for the incompetent Lionel, who cannot even collate his photocopying properly, than he deserves. He may be greatly wronged, the victim of a nasty trick such as only the Church could perpetrate and justify, but in the end, do we really care?

If recent writers have portrayed the clergy in a rather unfavorable and stereotyped light, their wives have fared even worse in both respects. Alan Ayckbourn's *Woman in Mind* opens with a scream of despair that echoes all the pent-up frustration of enduring a lifetime of second-hand sanctimoniousness. But Susan does not live up to the promise of this dramatic opening. Her despair, in the end, is reduced to sexual frustration and the petulance of an ignored child; her desires to the adolescent dreams of fame and fortune.

Alan Bennett's extended monologue, *A Bed Among the Lentils*, presents a similarly dismal picture. Here another Susan has retreated from the horrors of her loveless marriage (the only thing she can imagine that would be worse is being married to God) and flower arranging by becoming an alcoholic. A young Asian grocer, who owns the store where she buys her liquor, gives her the love her husband has denied her in his 'bed among the lentils'. It is he who persuades her to give up drink, but ironically, after he leaves, it is her husband who gets the credit. Indeed, she becomes the unwitting salvation of his faltering career as they become, on the after-dinner circuit, the ideal couple, having overcome all obstacles to enjoy an ideal and godly partnership.

These women end up hating the roles in which they find themselves, but unable to imagine any more original escape route than infidelity or alcohol.

Unfortunately, this fiction has some basis in reality. The rising incidence of clergy divorce and separation are the objective indicator of much unhappiness. The image of the clergyman who preaches the love of God to his flock but cannot communicate that love to his wife or children, is real as well as fictional. The clergy wife frustratingly bound by her role and unable or too frightened to escape from it is not just a playwright's fantasy.

One ex-clergy wife who identified herself as such turned up in the survey. Needless to say, she no longer attended church and classed herself as an agnostic. She now saw life as a 'series of chance events', but denied that this troubled her. Rather, it was a release. Those who had faith agonized, she claimed; those who had lost it did not.

If there is a correspondence between fiction and reality in these images of domestic clerical life, is there also one between the kinds of roles the Church is seen to play in the fiction discussed and the roles people expect it to play in reality? More specifically, do people perceive the Church as having any legitimate cultural role, or is the perception of the creative writers discussed above a fair one in this regard?

The survey sought to discover exactly how important people considered the 'cultural' roles of the Church to be in relation to various other roles it might play or be perceived to play. The choices, naturally, could not be absolutely comprehensive, but they did cover a wide spectrum ranging from personal salvation, through social and moral concerns, to cultural matters. There was also opportunity for respondents to name other roles under 'other', though relatively few did so and I was disappointed that those seemed often only to paraphrase answers already suggested in the questionnaire.

Overall, the highest mean score was for 'helping the poor and distressed' (3.47 on a scale of 1 to 4), thus giving some credence to David Hare's idealization of Lionel and ammunition to those who claim the Church has become nothing more than a glorified arm of the social services. Many of the 'write in' responses also reinforced this view of the Church. 'The social side – the community feel', and 'The Church should be a "drop in" place for everyone', were typical. The results correlated positively with frequency of church attendance, and there was also a marked positive correlation with education in a church-affiliated state school, in contrast to those educated in a church-affiliated independent school, 66% and 49% respectively.

This view of the Church was closely followed by 'conducting marriages and funerals' (3.39), which reinforces the results of the earlier question directed specifically at the importance of these services. Next in order of importance came 'a moral and ethical guide' (3.25), followed by the more individualistic and evangelical 'aiding individual salvation' (3.11). 'Preserving historic buildings' (2.94), was in fifth place, then 'commenting on social problems facing our country today' (2.90). Last of all, with a mean score of only 2.58, came 'maintaining and passing on a tradition of good music, art, and language'.

These are raw, overall scores. What they reveal is that in general people want a Church that provides the essential ceremonial for the major occasions of life and takes care of the social work side of things that the government seems to be doing less and less effectively. (This is not to denigrate 'caring for the poor and distressed', which is clearly part of Christ's charge to his followers. But it is as compatible with modern humanism as it is with Christianity; it need not be a specifically Christian or even religious role.)

People also want the Church to set moral standards though, as we shall see in the next chapter, the detailed questions in this area show that this concern is directed more to others than to themselves! They are less interested in it as a vehicle of divine grace leading to salvation in some future life. They

TABLE 4 *The importance of various roles of the Church (col. %)*

	Very important (4)	Fairly important (3)	Not very important (2)	Not at all important (1)	Don't know	Mean score
Total	614	614	614	614	614	
Aiding individual salvation	38	39	15	6	2	2.50
Commenting on social problems facing our country today	29	42	21	9	*	3.11
Maintaining and passing on a tradition of good music, art and language	16	37	36	11	*	2.90
Helping the poor and distressed	55	37	6	1	*	2.58
Moral and ethical guide	46	36	13	4	–	3.47
Preserving historic buildings	29	43	20	7	*	3.25
Conducting marriage and funerals	54	34	9	3	*	2.94
Other	6	2	*	*	92	3.39

* Less than 0.5

do not think that maintaining the fabric of churches is particularly important either unless they are agnostic. They are divided on whether they want the Church to comment on social problems, probably because while most people like what the Church has to say on *some* social issues, few are likely to be pleased with what it has to say on all. This also becomes clearer in the light of the responses analysed in the next chapter. Finally, they regard the Church's role in preserving its music, art, and liturgy as of very little importance at all.

What happens if, instead of looking at the overall scores, one concentrates on those who are Christian, and not only nominally but committed Christians, those who claim to attend church once a week or more? Most of the mean scores here are higher than the overall figures, as one would expect. More interesting is the change in priorities. 'Helping the poor and distressed' still ranks first, but 'moral and ethical guide' moves to number two from third position; 'aiding individual salvation' comes third rather than fourth, and the rather mechanical task of 'conducting marriages and funerals' drops from second to fourth place. If one compares denominations, it is Catholics who place most emphasis on the Church's role in individual salvation, while adherents of the Church of England place least.

Most significant for this study, however, is the placing of 'maintaining and passing on a tradition of good music, art, and language, and 'preserving historic buildings'. There is a major drop between the mean score of *all* the other options and these two, from 3.28 for the lowest of the others (commenting on social problems), to 2.67 and 2.57 for music and buildings respectively. Further, while in all other cases the committed respondents rated the roles significantly more important than the overall sample, here the difference is either small (2.67 for 'committed', as opposed to 2.58 overall) in the case of 'maintaining a tradition of good music', etc., or actually reversed in the case of 'preserving historic buildings' (2.57 for 'committed', 2.94 overall). Even more curiously, Nonconformists are more likely, by a small margin, to value music and liturgy than their traditionally liturgically-oriented counterparts in the Catholic Church and Church of England (mean score of 2.58 for both Catholics and C. of E., and of 2.68 for Nonconformists). The highest mean score by a significant margin for any subdivision on this question is for those educated in church-affiliated independent schools (2.89). Linking this to their very low score on 'caring for the poor and distressed' we again have an illustration of the way in which culture and caring Christianity appear to be dissociated from one another. (See Table 5.)

We can now see the apparently odd result with which this chapter began in context. What does it all mean?

Broadly, it would appear to mean that buildings, music, art, and liturgy are felt to be merely externals, peripheral to 'real religion', and that the more committed you are to Christianity, the more likely you are to feel that this is the case. Indeed, one does not have to seek far to hear just this message being proclaimed from numerous pulpits up and down the country. The final result dealing with the products of church-affiliated independent schools would seem to indicate that you only value these things if they have been presented to you as a child – but conversely, that if they *have* been presented to you, you do value them.

The breakdown according to schooling is overall most interesting and warrants more detailed examination. Of those who attended a non-denominational state school 12% rated 'maintaining and passing on a tradition of good music, art, and language', 'very important'; 11% of those from church-affiliated state schools; 19% from non-denominational independent schools, and 30% from church-affiliated independent schools. Thus those who went to a church-affiliated state school (and who score highly on questions measuring commitment) ranked *last* on the 'very important' response to this question. However, if you add together the 'very important' and 'fairly important' responses you get a different result: 47% non-denominational state schools, 62% church-affiliated state schools, 52% non-denominational independent schools, and 68% church-affiliated independent schools, showing, presumably, that those who went to church-affiliated state schools are more likely to place *some* value on the aesthetic aspects of worship, but are less likely to give it the high importance that at least *some* people educated in independent schools and non-denominational state schools do. It must be 'kept in its place'.

The greater value placed on the cultural and aesthetic

TABLE 5 *How important do you think it is that the Church play each of the following roles in Britain today? (col. %)*

	Total	DENOMINATION				BELIEF			RELIGIOUS UPBRINGING		RELIGIOUS ATTENDANCE				SCHOOLING			
		Catholic	C. of E.	Methodist	None	Christian	Agnostic	Atheist	Yes	No	Once week or more	Once month	Less often	Never	Non-den. state	Church-aff. state	Non-den. indep.	Church-aff. indep.
Total	614	60	350	76	94	385	142	78	332	281	161	87	192	174	371	70	93	79
Preserving historic buildings																		
Very important (+4)	29	22	33	32	32	26	37	29	25	33	17	31	35	32	26	23	30	46
Fairly important (+3)	43	45	43	43	52	41	46	53	46	40	37	51	40	49	45	39	47	35
Not very important (+2)	20	23	17	25	14	23	15	12	20	20	31	14	18	15	21	23	19	13
Not at all important (+1)	7	10	7	9	2	10	2	5	9	5	15	5	6	3	7	14	3	6
Don't know	*	–	1	–	–	*	–	1	–	1	–	–	1	1	*	1	–	–
Mean score	2.94	2.78	3.03	2.79	3.14	2.84	3.17	3.08	2.87	3.03	2.57	3.08	3.06	3.10	2.90	2.71	3.04	3.20

Maintaining and passing on a tradition of good music, art and language

Very important (+4)	16	13	16	17	18	16	16	15	19	12	18	20	15	12	12	11	19	30
Fairly important (+3)	37	40	36	39	36	39	35	31	40	35	38	40	35	37	35	51	33	38
Not very important (+2)	36	38	37	38	29	36	39	29	32	40	37	30	36	36	40	33	33	22
Not at all important (+1)	11	8	11	5	17	9	9	24	10	12	7	9	13	14	12	4	13	10
Don't know	*	–	1	–	–	1	1	–	–	1	–	1	1	1	1	–	1	–
Mean score	2.58	2.58	2.58	2.68	2.55	2.62	2.59	2.37	2.67	2.47	2.67	2.71	2.53	2.48	2.49	2.70	2.60	2.89

* Less than 0.5

aspects of religion by those who have attended church-affiliated independent schools, coupled with their greater knowledge of these things (see chapter 2), seems to show that the
'myth' of the divided society is still all too clearly a reality.
And the thesis, put forward in the previous chapter, that one
is most likely to value what one knows and has been exposed
to, is further supported. What kind of school a child attends
will have a direct bearing on whether he or she knows and
values traditional church music, art, and liturgy.

Whether knowing and valuing these things is of importance
either to society at large or to personal religious development
is more debatable. We have discovered that most people who
consider themselves committed Christians think they are not,
and that conversely those edcucated in church-affiliated
independent schools, who think they are, rate low on other
measures of commitment. Further, it is well known that the
variety of Christianity that is expanding most rapidly in
England today is precisely that which seeks least relationship
with the historical Church in all its aspects.

Here I wish to return to a distinction made in the first
chapter between the 'historical' Church (that developed in its
richness in late antiquity and throughout the Middle Ages,
the Church of creeds, liturgies, music, and ceremonial) and
the primitive Church, which demanded an unmediated
response to Christ as Saviour and Lord. These two ancient
divisions are reflected in two dominant types of Christianity
today.

What I shall label the 'unhistorical' type of Christianity
was both legitimate and inevitable as it existed in the first
century. Today it may be a different matter. Lord Rees-Mogg,
in my interview with him, spoke of the 'attempt to re-create
Jesus as if he were a contemporary of ours' as being 'rather
like virtual reality in the new computer work . . . it's trying
to get over the difficulty of the historical gap by creating an
image which seems to me to be very remote from any reality.'
And Lord Runcie also referred with some unease to 'a sense
of bringing people to Christ in an individualistic way which
seems to sell them the whole package, and they don't feel you
need anything between Jesus and today'.

The historical/unhistorical divisions in modern church
practice now cut across denominational boundaries, so that

one can have, for example, Catholic services that eschew the
traditions of the past altogether and Nonconformist services
that incorporate a high degree of ritual and tradition. The
Church of England is split with the Anglo-Catholic wing at
one exteme and the new Evangelical and charismatic congregations that are mushrooming everywhere at the other, and
with most of the Church doing its usual delicate balancing
act trying to keep everyone happy.

There may be good arguments for some elements of the
'unhistorical' kind of worship. Certainly, an immediate
relationship with Christ, for those who have found it and can
sustain it in their personal lives, is a great gift. However, the
sense of a surviving, living community of believers stretching
back through the centuries, using the same words, the same
images to express that faith, provides sustenance for the faith
of many others. The past, as argued in chapter 1, implies a
future. Immediacy implies or predicts nothing outside
immediacy.

Within the practice of Christian worship there are two
further divisions: that of simplicity and that of ornateness.
These divisions sometimes coincide with those between what
I have described as 'historical' and 'unhistorical' worship, but
they do not necessarily do so, and there is good philosophical
and aesthetic justification for both schools of thought.

Briefly, the 'simple' style of worship, found in its purest
form among the Quakers and the Shakers in America, argues
that earthly objects – art and music – no matter how perfect,
are a distraction, coming between people and God and that,
further, they engender the sin of pride as men and women
concentrate on the cleverness of their own constructs and
forget the maker of all. The ornate and baroque forms of
worship are justified on the grounds that people are helped
to reach God through mediate, earthly forms of perfection
and should offer these to God, the author of all beauty, as the
best human reflection of that beauty.

These two theologies and aesthetics both have a long and
ancient history. To some extent which one responds to is
probably a matter of temperament, though the same person
can respond to the appeal of both. George Herbert, for
example, who advocated the plain style in the writing of

religious poetry, walked to Salisbury Cathedral every Sunday evening to glory in the worship and music he found there.

What seems more difficult to justify, however, is the careless and plain bad (by any standards) worship that seems to characterize much of the Church today. Whatever happens in Church, surely, should be designed to move, inspire, and uplift. I use the word 'designed' deliberately, because much of current worship seems just to happen; whether it is Prayer Book or ASB or some relatively unstructured modern service, nothing seems 'designed' to do anything. I have attended Anglo-Catholic services where servers were incompetent and clergy shambolic, including one where an altar vessel, after numerous near misses, was actually knocked over. I have attended an Evangelical service where the rite of Baptism by immersion, potentially most moving, was deflated in seriousness and importance by remarks such as 'Isn't she good-looking?' – made about one of the female candidates, of course. One can get the impression that presentation simply doesn't matter.

It was Michael Mayne who offered the only tentative explanation for this situation, which he agreed existed. 'A lot of clergy, I think, are possibly dispirited, possibly bored, possibly threatened.' But David Edwards, Provost of Southwark, in a completely tangential observation, may have shed even more light on the situation. 'Congregations . . . (is this not the case?) prefer in a preacher the sense that he's sort of thinking aloud and stumbling'. Then, referring to his work with the BBC, he revealed that although the script is in front of you they 'often encourage you . . . to half stumble over the words . . . in order to try and make it seem spontaneous'.

Here we have an aesthetic theory, put forward (possibly unwittingly) by no less powerful an authority than the BBC, that what appears spontaneous, amateur, is what is most likely to appeal. So is the casual, unplanned nature of much modern worship deliberately so because it is believed that this is what most people will readily relate to? And if this is true, why? Is the alternating build-up and deflation I witnessed in the Evangelical church a sign that people are *afraid* of greatness, afraid of being moved, inspired, uplifted? Do we stick with the comfortable, the friendly, the mundane because it is where we feel most at home?

Outside the bounds of the main-line churches altogether the sects, particularly the American imports, do it rather differently. Here things are done 'well', in their own terms. The television broadcasts of the major Evangelical figures and their personal crusades are models of slickness. Emotions *are* manipulated, for better or worse: some, even among the Evangelical wing of the Church of England, believe for worse. John Irvine, explaining the somewhat low-key approach of worship at St Barnabas, Kensington, says, 'I'm not wanting to leave emotions out, but I do think that they are powerful things and it is important that those who lead worship don't manipulate emotions'. Such scruples do not appear to extend to most of the new independent sects and, indeed, once one leaves the area of traditional liturgy it is very difficult to achieve a balance between worship that is well done but not 'slick'; moving, but not 'manipulative'.

What is indisputable is that it is a fundamentalist form of Christianity, rejecting traditional forms of worship, that is gaining ground most rapidly in England today. An in-depth analysis of the reasons for this trend is far beyond the scope of this study, but the survey results do suggest some possibilities. It is also the form of Christianity that makes least demands on the worshipper in terms of cultural knowledge. Is the ease of access to this form of Christianity part of its attraction, and has this increased as the difficulty of access to traditional forms of worship increases because of the documented wide-spread ignorance of both its form and content? Is ours a society that values this 'ease' above all else, that believes if it can't be made simple it isn't worth bothering about? And is the emphasis on the total solution of life's problems, the simplistic understanding of conversion, another form of ease which clinches the attractiveness of the total package? This is speculation, not assertion, but it is speculation rooted in some statistical fact and rather more observation.

It is also supported by the recent comments of various church figures. The Vicar of Harold Wood, quoted in an article on the 'Jesus Army', sounds rather like the fictional Bishop of Salisbury in Susan Howatch's novel. He warns, 'There's a danger of a thirst for the supernatural rather than a thirst for God'. He speaks of a 'real hunger', and says, 'I'm concerned the hunger is [should be] satisfied with something substantial and people are not let down'.[5]

Ironically, the Church of England itself seems engaged in this process of 'letting down'. Obsessed with eradicating what it believes to be an image that is 'bound to a suburban or middle class culture' and 'its own special ecclesiastical culture',[6] it has, within the last decade, undergone some soul searching about what is required to reach those who have not known its influence from childhood. The recent report of the Church of England's theological advisory group, *Good News in our Times* is concerned that:

> to the outsider people in church . . . appear to think in a funny way. The focus of their thoughts always seems to be in the past. They are always using concepts which do not seem to be rooted in everyday experience. This makes them appear not merely 'odd' but largely irrelevant.[7]

One cannot argue with the position that the Church and its trappings are now alien to most people. The results of the survey that I have quoted prove that beyond doubt. Further, they prove that this is so not only among the working class, but among well-educated professionals. But need it be axiomatic that the Church therefore should change so as to become something 'familiar' to most people, instantly 'relevant'?[8] What kind of religion would it be that was exclusively (or even primarily) 'rooted in everyday experience'? Everyday experience, surely, is what we need religion to help us endure and make sense of. All those people in the survey who agreed that 'sorrow and suffering make sense within a larger pattern' (53%) are surely seeking (or possibly have found) that larger pattern.

A religion that brings God down to man without also raising man up to God is a peculiarly modern notion. Immanence without transcendence must in the end prove barren – an incarnation without an ascension, God sharing our pain but denying us a vision of his glory. The comfortable human things – the clasp of the hand, the touch of sympathy, the listening ear – all have their importance. They may, done in the name of Christ, be Christian. But they need not be so; they are not intrinsically so; they are not even intrinsically religious. The exceptionally high value placed on these things in people's assessment of the role of the Church in the survey seems to show that we have lost sight of what is essentially religious and what is accidentally so.

The critic may at this point say I am misunderstanding – deliberately misunderstanding. What should be made familiar and comfortable to people who enter the Church from outside is not essential doctrine but the paraphernalia. Yet how can the two be divorced in this way, when the 'paraphernalia' implicitly conveys the doctrine, states it in a hundred ways from the obvious, like Church architecture and the liturgy, to the obscure, the smallest gesture of priest and worshipper? You cannot divorce 'the tongue from the heart', the external from the internal. A Church that uses only common language, ordinary music, can scarcely raise a more than common hope in its adherents.

'Worship', said Lord Runcie, 'shows us where our values and hearts lie. . . It must be something which is about God, and not chiefly about ourselves, and any act of worship would . . . need to elevate us rather than to comfort or to be a means of self-expression. Therefore traditions of worship should always be above people's heads rather than beneath their feet – and must communicate transcendent religion.'

If this is the case (and many will not concede that it is), must those brought up outside the Church, to whom these thing are not familiar from childhood, be doomed to be perpetual outcasts? It is frequently said that the Church must meet people where they are, and given that otherwise no communication at all will take place (one can scarcely meet people where they are *not* either literally or figuratively) this seems a truism. What I question is the implicit axiom, which is that the Church must not only meet them there but leave them there. This seems much more dubious.

Again Lord Runcie, having characterized the rewriting of 'ancient texts of great beauty in a way which makes them flat and wooden', as 'grievous', continues:

> And however much people may say, 'O well the children understand it' – but I ask the question, 'Are they being nourished to enter into something bigger than themselves

and are they being fed with hallowed words which will stand them in good stead in times of difficulty or joy?'

This raises the whole Christian notion of initiation – people being 'nourished to enter into something bigger than themselves'. But where is this tradition of initiation to be found in the Church at large today? We still speak of baptism and confirmation as 'initiation rites', but too often the practice of preparing the convert for initiation, taken very seriously in the early Church, is cut short or by-passed, so that what we are left with is an initiation rite that is just that – a rite.

The problems of religious education in the schools of what is now a multi-cultural society are manifold, but what of the Church's own mission to educate? When even faithful members of the Church of many years' standing are ignorant of the basics of the faith, never mind the significance of much of the liturgy and worship, no wonder it seems to assume that the only possibility with potential converts is to accept their state of knowledge as a 'given'. Is there any justification in Christian theology for this complacency? Christ may have selected uneducated fishermen as his disciples, but he took the task of teaching them quite seriously. If the results of the survey reflect generally on society at large, surely they reflect specifically on the Church.

What seems to be happening instead of this 'raising' of knowledge and awareness is a reduction of everything to the lowest common denominator. From those who gave you the Good News Bible (intended, incidentally, for those whose first language was not English), we are now to receive a further offering described as 'a scripture for the Bart Simpson generation'. This 'translation' reduces such concepts as the grace of God to 'But God is really kind'.[9] Who decides that 'ordinary' people are not able to understand the concept of 'grace'? And, even on a secular level, what child who cannot understand it can read *Measure for Measure*, what teacher can teach it?

One can extend the concept of 'initiation' beyond matters of doctrine to Church practice and worship. Enabling people to enjoy what is 'best' in Church music, art, and liturgy and literature, is surely one specific example of the general Platonic notion that it is through appreciation of earthly beauty that we rise to heavenly things. If God is perfection, then our response to him should be that which, in earthly terms, most nearly reaches that perfection.

I should emphasize that 'most nearly perfect' does mean that and not just 'more ancient', an impression that a superficial reading of the preceding chapters might seem to convey. Everything written more than one hundred years ago is not sacrosanct, as Stephen Darlington, organist of Christ Church Cathedral, Oxford, impressed upon me when I spoke to him. 'Cathedrals themselves, cathedral musicians, have not helped matters by putting on bad music. Let's face it, a lot of the Victorian stuff is absolute rubbish.' If this 'rubbish' is the best the Church has to put against the banalities of some of the modern alternatives, its case is indeed wholly lost.

This argument is based firmly on the position (widely disputed) that there is better and worse and that this is discoverable by human taste and reason. It also takes the optimistic view that, given the proper exposure, most people will recognize the good when it is presented to them, when they are 'initiated'.

As for those who deny a hierarchy in the arts, and resist the hierarchical implications (different from condescension) of the teachers and the taught, the initiators and the initiates, one can only reply that anyone who denies hierarchy as a principle comes dangerously close to denying the existence of any God recognizable by Christianity. However much one may wish to 'universalize' Christianity, to free it from any cultural moorings, certain principles that may be seen as culturally induced are so intrinsic to its fundamental doctrine that it is difficult to imagine their eradication. If there is no hierarchy, how is God himself 'above' us in any sense, an object of worship? One returns again to my agnostic colleague who argued that value judgements of any kind are ultimately dependent on belief in a supreme being – and made impossible by lack of such a belief.

It is possible, of course, to ignore the philosophical implications and take the salesperson's approach. 'Better' or 'worse', whether or not existent in any absolute sense, are irrelevant. 'Better' is what attracts in immediate terms; 'worse' is what, in Lionel's words quoted at the beginning of this chapter, 'puts [people] off', 'sets up a resistance'. Everything is reduced to the lowest common denominator because we believe this is what will attract people, what will sell. On a purely commercial basis this may be eminently sensible, but it does seem to involve a profound contempt for the customer. One would hope that the Church might retain different human values and criteria of success.

The ultimate tragedy of the division I perceive between Christianity and culture is that it refuses to recognize the interconnection between the two. Argument from autobiography is always suspect, but just as my first experience of textual comparison came through the Bible, so my first recalled aesthetic experiences came chiefly through the Church – a church with a liturgy, but very definitely not pretentious or 'high'. The words alone were enough. 'Let my prayer be set forth before Thee as incense' was moving before its meaning was known. The petition 'That we may walk in a perfect heart', set to Farrant's music, is still indelibly set against the snow-white background of a Canadian winter.

Of course, beauty does not always inspire faith; it may remain an end in itself. My friend who responded so dramatically to the opening chorus of the 'St Matthew Passion' did not therefore become a Christian. But sometimes it may so inspire. Surely the chance alone is enough to persuade us not to divorce it from the Church. One of my follow-up interviews took me to see a young man at a Cambridge college with a strong musical tradition. I had selected him because his knowledge of music was clearly unusual, and his general answers were also well above average. As I approached his room it occurred to me that I could guess why he had done so well – he was a choral scholar. I was right, but, it emerged, he was also a committed, practising Christian, and he was among those few practising Christians who had *not* been 'religiously brought up' at home. When asked how he had come to the Church he said that it was through the combination of his school (independent) and music.

After this real life example, one final fictional one. In the Booker Prize novel *Moon Tiger* the narrator, a former journalist who is dying in hospital while contemplating writing a 'history of the world', comments thus on churches and cathedrals: 'They are intended to uplift and terrify. They are an argument made manifest.'

The argument is another matter. What I am trying to demonstrate at this point is the amazing legacy of God – or the possibility of God – by way not of ideas but of manipulation of the landscape. Churches have always seemed to me almost irrefutable evidence. They make me wonder if – just possibly – I might be wrong.[10]

The Church ignores these 'arguments made manifest' – churches, music, poetry – at its peril. In the end they may prove to be not just 'externals', 'paraphernalia', but those things that show us what at our best we truly are – or could be.

4

MORALS AND MEANING

I think it's really true that a lot of people just don't know that chastity has been reckoned to be quite a good thing. I mean, it doesn't occur to them.

David Edwards, Provost of Southwark

A religion is not only about worship, prayer, and the elevation of the human spirit; it is also about how we live our lives here and now. Nor should the two be disconnected. Words and actions implicitly reveal what we think life is about and where we are going. They are, consciously or unconsciously, the embodiment of a philosophy of life.

How one discovers and measures these things with any accuracy is a problem, and numerous difficulties emerged in this part of the survey. First of all, what one is measuring can only be the conscious part of moral behaviour. And we know that frequently this is at variance with what people actually do, the priorities they establish in the use of their time and money, which are probably the true keys to their values. In many of the questions one is dealing with the respondent's self-perception, which cannot be verified in any objective way.

More profound in its implications is the lack of agreement about what the moral vocabulary means. Because of this the objective questions present themselves subjectively in different forms to different respondents. 'Sin', for example, is a definable theological term, but it means widely different things to people in our society today, ranging from only the most heinous crimes to the first stirrings of selfish impulse in the infant. And, as will be discussed below, a good many people believe the very concept is meaningless – for them wrongdoing has ceased to have a theological dimension at all.

Bearing these limitations in mind, the survey attempted to

discover what the chief moral influence in one's life is likely to have been and to what extent people in England today still adhere to Christian standards of morality, whether or not they are practising Christians. (See Table 6.)

In relation to the first question, the home emerged as the chief moral influence by a very large margin. (Church, home, and teacher or friend were the suggested categories, with the opportunity to write in under 'other'.) This is consistent with the arguments of contemporary philosophers such as Berger who see one of the results of secularization as a retreat of religion and religious values from society as a whole to the family. Overall, 76% claimed the home as their greatest moral influence, 7% the Church, and 6% a teacher or friend. Even among Christians, those citing the Church rose to only 10%.

Those who rated the home lowest were those who attended church-affiliated independent schools; only 56% of these people claimed the home as their greatest moral influence, and the rating of 'teacher and friend' and 'other' was correspondingly high (16% and 18% respectively). Rather curiously, those who attended non-denominational independent schools displayed a very different pattern with 77% rating the family as their chief moral influence and only 2% a 'teacher or friend'. There are at least two possible interpretations of this significant difference between denominational and non-denominational independent schools. One is that the denominational schools exert a much greater moral influence on their charges than the non-denominational ones with a resultant weakening of the influence of family. The other is that the non-denominational independent schools are predominantly day schools and the denominational ones boarding schools, and that this, rather than their religious or non-religious character, is the chief variable.

There is certainly nothing intrinsically wrong with the home being the chief moral influence in one's life. Indeed, it *could* be the ideal answer. However, when one couples these figures with those to the question 'Were you brought up religiously at home?' discussed in chapter 2, the implications look somewhat worrying. Overall 54% replied 'yes' to this question, but the figure rose to 64% for teachers and professionals (mostly over 30) and fell to 35% for first-year university students. Given that this is a question about a past objective fact rather than

TABLE 6 *What or whom would you say has been the greatest moral influence in your life? (col. %)*

	Total	DENOMINATION				BELIEF			RELIGIOUS UPBRINGING		RELIGIOUS ATTENDANCE				SCHOOLING			
		Cath-olic	C. of E.	Metho-dist	None	Chris-tian	Agno-stic	Athe-ist	Yes	No	Once week or more	Once month	Less often	Never	Non-den. state	Church-aff. state	Non-den. indep.	Church-aff. indep.
Total	614	60	350	76	94	385	142	78	332	281	161	87	192	174	371	70	93	79
The Church	7	7	7	7	2	10	2	–	7	7	14	15	1	3	7	10	6	4
Home (parents, brothers, sisters, uncles etc.)	76	72	78	74	80	73	81	81	76	76	63	71	84	80	81	69	77	56
Teacher, or friend	6	7	7	5	2	7	3	4	5	7	6	6	5	6	4	7	2	16
Other	8	8	6	12	12	7	11	9	9	8	14	5	5	9	6	10	10	18
Don't know	3	7	2	3	4	3	4	6	4	2	2	2	5	3	2	4	4	6

an attitude, where ideas among the young may change with age, it seems difficult to escape the conclusion that the home, the chief moral influence, is significantly less a *Christian* moral influence than it has been in the past, and that this will affect the ideas and beliefs of the coming generation. Everything else we know about the family would corroborate this finding, and the responses of the students to the rest of the survey indicate that its effects are already much in evidence. It is also corroborated by the Gallup *Values* survey (July 1990) which asked the same question of a cross-section of the general population. The replies here, broken down by ten-year age bands, show a steady decline in religious upbringing from the older to the younger respondents, with only one hiccup in the 55–64 age band.

With regard to the second aim of this part of the survey (measuring the extent to which moral attitudes are still fundamentally Christian) the subjective element was a major difficulty. If you ask individuals whether their actions in private life in general conform with Christian morality, the response you get depends on (a) how honest they are prepared to be about their own lives and (b) what they perceive Christian morality to be. Certain other questions tried to measure the latter indirectly, but any that were penetrating in a personal way – even in the follow-up interviews – would have been an unacceptable invasion of privacy.

Bearing in mind these reservations, the poll found that overall 80% of people believe that 'most of [their] actions in private life fit in with Christian morality'. Asked the same question in relation to public life (that is work/official dealings), 83%, an even higher number, said they did so. If one excludes students, who on both counts were well below teachers and professionals in a positive response, the percentages rise to an astonishing 91% and 92% (figures for students are 59% in private life, 64% in public life). (See Table 7.)

If we take these figures at face value there is great cause for optimism. If over 90% of the professionals of this country apply Christian standards to both their private and public actions this must be the most godly society since at least the seventeenth century. Even 65% of atheists and 70% of those who claim never to go to church respond positively to this question.

TABLE 7 *Please tell me whether you agree or disagree with the following statements (col. %)*

		SAMPLE GROUP			SEX		SUBJECTS			QUALIFICATIONS					POLITICS		SEES LIFE AS	
	Total	Stud-ents	Teach-ers	Profes-sionals	Male	Female	Scien-ces	Appl. Scien-ces	Arts	Vocat-ional	Post grad.	Degree	Dip-loma/ 'A' level	Other	Left	Right	Mean-ingful patt.	Chance series of events
Total	614	205	214	195	388	226	159	88	188	198	136	319	141	17	253	298	357	183
Most of my actions in private life fit in with Christian morality																		
Agree	80	59	91	91	81	79	81	81	76	85	92	71	91	76	76	84	85	71
Disagree	17	36	7	7	15	19	16	14	23	12	5	25	9	18	21	14	13	26
Don't know	3	5	1	2	4	2	3	6	1	4	3	4	1	6	3	2	2	3
In difficult situations I consciously try to take a Christian perspective into account before I speak or act																		
Agree	50	25	58	67	51	48	44	50	49	59	60	40	60	65	42	55	64	27
Disagree	45	68	36	30	44	46	49	43	48	36	35	54	37	35	54	39	31	69
Don't know	5	7	5	3	5	6	7	7	3	5	6	6	4	–	4	6	5	4
Christian morality has no bearing on the way I behave																		
Agree	15	25	12	8	13	19	14	18	18	12	11	20	9	12	19	12	9	27
Disagree	81	67	86	89	83	77	81	80	78	85	85	76	89	76	76	85	89	65
Don't know	4	7	2	3	4	4	6	2	4	3	4	4	2	12	5	3	2	8

	Total	DENOMINATION				BELIEF			RELIGIOUS UPBRINGING		RELIGIOUS ATTENDANCE				SCHOOLING			
		Cath-olic	C. of E.	Metho-dist	None	Chris-tian	Agno-stic	Athe-ist	Yes	No	Once week or more	Once month	Less often	Never	Non-den. state	Church-aff. state	Non-den. indep.	Church-aff. indep.
Total	614	60	350	76	94	385	142	78	332	281	161	87	192	174	371	70	93	79

Most of my actions in private life fit in with Christian morality

	Total	Cath-olic	C. of E.	Metho-dist	None	Chris-tian	Agno-stic	Athe-ist	Yes	No	Once week or more	Once month	Less often	Never	Non-den. state	Church-aff. state	Non-den. indep.	Church-aff. indep.
Agree	80	77	80	91	72	87	73	65	86	73	94	90	74	70	81	79	73	84
Disagree	17	22	17	8	22	11	24	28	13	22	5	9	23	25	16	19	22	15
Don't know	3	2	3	1	5	2	4	6	1	5	1	1	3	6	3	3	5	1

In difficult situations I consciously try to take a Christian perspective into account before I speak or act

	Total	Cath-olic	C. of E.	Metho-dist	None	Chris-tian	Agno-stic	Athe-ist	Yes	No	Once week or more	Once month	Less often	Never	Non-den. state	Church-aff. state	Non-den. indep.	Church-aff. indep.
Agree	50	53	52	78	10	68	22	17	64	34	82	62	41	24	51	57	46	43
Disagree	45	43	42	18	85	27	74	79	33	59	16	29	52	72	45	37	47	49
Don't know	5	3	6	4	5	5	4	4	4	7	2	9	7	5	4	6	6	8

Christian morality has no bearing on the way I behave

	Total	Cath-olic	C. of E.	Metho-dist	None	Chris-tian	Agno-stic	Athe-ist	Yes	No	Once week or more	Once month	Less often	Never	Non-den. state	Church-aff. state	Non-den. indep.	Church-aff. indep.
Agree	15	13	15	3	29	7	25	33	10	21	3	5	16	31	14	11	18	22
Disagree	81	83	81	95	64	92	68	55	87	73	96	93	80	62	82	89	78	72
Don't know	4	3	4	3	7	1	7	12	3	5	1	2	4	7	4	–	3	6

One must ask, however, to what extent these results are conditioned by what is a socially acceptable response. Even faced with an anonymous interviewer, and guaranteed personal anonymity, will a school teacher or an eminent professional admit to *not* living a life that, in general, conforms to Christian morality? Is the reason that students rate themselves so much less highly in answer to this question really that they lead substantially less moral lives than their elders or simply that it is more socially acceptable in that milieu to admit to deviation from 'correct' standards? Further, what do the respondents classify as 'non-Christian' morality?

This last question is posed particularly in relation to the rather curious differences of the three major church groupings. If one is to take the results of the survey straight, Roman Catholics are much greater sinners than Church of England adherents, and Nonconformists are the most righteous of the lot. (The figures for 'actions in private life' are 77%, 80% and 91% respectively; for 'actions in public life' they are 77%, 84% and 95%.)

What does one make of this? It seems to me that the differences here are not in *actual* behaviour but in standards of behaviour set and in the rigorousness with which they are applied to the self. In the case of Roman Catholics, it is known that large numbers of couples do not adhere to the official teaching of the Church regarding birth control. Do at least some of them, therefore, regard themselves as *not* adhering to standards of Christian morality in private life in an area where either Church of England or Nonconformists, acting in the same way, would suffer no feelings of guilt at all? Further, does the emphasis of the Catholic Church on confession instil a feeling of guilt in its members that adherents of other denominations escape?

What is more difficult to explain is why Nonconformists, with their traditional emphasis on the individual examination of conscience, feel the most self-righteous. One might assume that we are seeing here the effects of the optimistic, 'easy' Christianity of the fringe groups (and increasingly certain main-line churches), who emphasize the love of God to the exclusion of judgement, or that we are looking at a group of people who have a very broad definition of what is 'right' and a very narrow one of what is 'wrong' – that is, if you do not murder, steal, or beat your wife nightly you are a pretty good person. But their response to the follow-up question, 'In difficult situations I consciously try to take a Christian perspective into account before I speak or act' negates these possibilities. While only 50% overall responded 'yes' to this statement (68% of all Christians), 78% of Nonconformists did so. This is in marked contrast to only 53% of Catholics and 52% of Anglicans. It would seem therefore that Nonconformists do, on the basis of their own assessment, live more closely by Christian rules than either Catholics or Church of England. Perhaps this does indicate a survival of the tradition of self-examination according to individual conscience in these churches, but it is impossible on the available evidence to be sure.

The general discrepancy between the answers to whether one lives in conformity with Christian morality and whether one *consciously* takes a Christian perspective into account when speaking or acting would indicate that for the majority of people Christian behaviour is assumed rather than consciously examined. Indeed, the very high percentages in response to the first question would seem to indicate that it is pretty easy, in the view of most people, to live a morally impeccable life. David Edwards suggests that we have moved so far from a consciously examined morality that it is 'really true that a lot of people just don't know that chastity ever has been reckoned to be quite a good thing. I mean it doesn't occur to them.'

There is, naturally, a positive correlation between Christian commitment, church attendance, and religious upbringing on both these questions. The results relating to schooling are less predictable. Those who attended church-affiliated independent schools are most likely to believe their actions in private life fit in with Christian morality (84%), followed by those from non-denominational state schools (81%). But in response to the second question concerning conscious Christian speech and action, those from church-affiliated state schools scored highest (57%) while those from church-affiliated independent schools were lowest (43%).

Does this suggest that those from the church-affiliated independent schools are more ready to *assume* they behave well, while those from church-affiliated state schools are more likely to examine their behaviour in a critical way? What is clear is that there is an inverse correlation between the low response to the question on conscious Christian action from the church-affiliated independent schools and their very positive response to the questions in the previous chapter dealing with knowledge of church liturgy and music as well as the value placed upon it. This reinforces the impression that things that ought to be complementary have somehow become divorced in a very unfortunate way. Truth and beauty, goodness and aesthetic appreciation may not be the natural companions poets and artists have imagined.

The follow-up questions to the second statement (that actions in public life fit in with Christian morality) received an even lower positive response. Asked whether they measured the government's actions against Christian standards, only 32% agreed that they did so (43% of Christians). Here again the Nonconformists scored highest with 47% in contrast to 42% of Roman Catholics and a mere 30% of Church of England. Only 35% overall said that the way they voted was influenced by the actions of the political parties judged by Christian standards, and this percentage rose to only 65% among those who claimed to attend church once a week or more. Again those from independent schools (either non-denominational or church-affiliated) were *less* likely to measure the government's actions or have their voting affected by Christian standards than those who attended state schools. So our politicians can rest largely untroubled by what the churches think of their doings! The implications of this apparent divorce between religion and government, even among those who claim to be Christian, will be looked at again in the next chapter.

Despite all of the above, when asked whether the Church should give guidance on personal issues such as abortion, marriage and divorce, extra-marital affairs, homosexuality, and euthanasia, the majority of people thought it should. Percentages varied considerably with the particular issue concerned. Marriage and divorce ranked highest (77%), followed by extra-marital affairs and euthanasia (both 64%) and abortion (63%). Homosexuality ranked last, with only a small majority (56%) believing the Church should give guidance on this matter. The ranking may reflect either the extent to

TABLE 8 *Attitude statements (col. %)*

	Total	DENOMINATION				BELIEF			RELIGIOUS UPBRINGING		RELIGIOUS ATTENDANCE				SCHOOLING			
		Cath-olic	C. of E.	Metho-dist	None	Chris-tian	Agno-stic	Athe-ist	Yes	No	Once week or more	Once month	Less often	Never	Non-den. state	Church-aff. state	Non-den. indep.	Church-aff. indep.
Total	614	60	350	76	94	385	142	78	332	281	161	87	192	174	371	70	93	79

Most of my actions in public life (that is, work/official dealings) fit in with Christian morality

	Total	Cath-olic	C. of E.	Metho-dist	None	Chris-tian	Agno-stic	Athe-ist	Yes	No	Once week or more	Once month	Less often	Never	Non-den. state	Church-aff. state	Non-den. indep.	Church-aff. indep.
Agree	83	77	84	95	67	89	77	63	88	76	96	87	81	70	85	81	93	76
Disagree	12	17	11	5	20	7	15	27	10	15	2	10	13	20	11	16	9	16
Don't know	5	7	5	–	13	3	8	10	2	9	2	2	6	10	4	3	11	8

I usually measure the government's actions against Christian standards, and judge them accordingly

	Total	Cath-olic	C. of E.	Metho-dist	None	Chris-tian	Agno-stic	Athe-ist	Yes	No	Once week or more	Once month	Less often	Never	Non-den. state	Church-aff. state	Non-den. indep.	Church-aff. indep.
Agree	32	42	30	47	14	43	18	10	40	23	58	30	23	20	35	37	26	24
Disagree	63	53	66	46	81	52	80	85	55	72	38	69	70	76	61	54	71	72
Don't know	5	5	4	7	5	5	3	5	5	5	4	1	7	5	5	9	3	4

The way I vote is influenced by the actions of the political parties judged by Christian standards

	Total	Cath-olic	C. of E.	Metho-dist	None	Chris-tian	Agno-stic	Athe-ist	Yes	No	Once week or more	Once month	Less often	Never	Non-den. state	Church-aff. state	Non-den. indep.	Church-aff. indep.
Agree	35	47	33	49	14	48	18	10	45	24	65	38	24	18	35	50	27	34
Disagree	61	53	63	46	84	48	80	86	51	72	30	59	71	80	61	50	65	63
Don't know	4	–	5	5	2	5	1	4	4	4	5	3	5	2	4	–	9	3

TABLE 9 *Do you believe the Church should give guidance on personal issues such as . . . ? (col. %)*

		SAMPLE GROUP			SEX		SUBJECTS				QUALIFICATIONS				POLITICS		SEES LIFE AS	
	Total	Stud-ents	Teach-ers	Profes-sionals	Male	Female	Scien-ces	Appl. Scien-ces	Arts	Voca-tional	Post grad.	Degree	Dip-loma/'A' level	Other	Left	Right	Mean-ingful patt.	Chance series of events
Total	614	205	214	195	388	226	159	88	188	198	136	319	141	17	253	298	357	183
Abortion																		
Yes	63	49	69	70	70	50	58	59	60	71	68	60	67	53	57	67	71	46
No	35	50	29	27	28	48	40	39	38	27	29	39	32	35	41	31	27	52
Don't know	2	1	2	3	2	2	2	2	2	2	3	1	1	12	2	2	2	2
Marriage and divorce																		
Yes	77	66	80	84	82	68	75	76	71	83	81	73	82	76	70	80	84	62
No	22	34	18	15	18	31	23	23	29	16	18	26	18	24	29	19	15	37
Extra-marital affairs																		
Yes	64	50	70	72	69	55	63	64	60	70	71	61	66	53	60	66	73	50
No	34	49	27	25	28	42	35	35	39	25	26	38	28	41	39	31	25	48
Homosexuality																		
Yes	56	36	65	68	64	42	55	51	53	65	68	50	60	41	51	60	68	38
No	41	60	33	29	33	54	42	47	45	32	30	46	37	47	47	36	29	61
Euthanasia																		
Yes	64	45	73	75	69	55	63	55	62	73	73	57	72	59	59	67	73	49
No	33	51	23	23	28	41	35	41	37	22	22	39	27	35	38	29	23	48

	Total	DENOMINATION				BELIEF			RELIGIOUS UPBRINGING		RELIGIOUS ATTENDANCE				SCHOOLING			
		Cath-olic	C. of E.	Metho-dist	None	Chris-tian	Agno-stic	Athe-ist	Yes	No	Once week or more	Once month	Less often	Never	Non-den. state	Church -aff. state	Non-den. indep.	Church -aff. indep.
Total	614	60	350	76	94	385	142	78	332	281	161	87	192	174	371	70	93	79
Abortion																		
Yes	63	70	62	72	48	73	47	44	70	54	88	67	57	44	59	70	67	71
No	35	25	36	26	52	25	49	56	27	44	11	31	42	53	39	29	33	27
Don't know	2	5	2	1	–	2	4	–	2	1	1	2	1	3	2	1	–	3
Marriage and divorce																		
Yes	77	80	76	89	62	85	63	63	84	68	94	84	73	60	74	83	78	78
No	22	18	23	9	36	14	36	37	15	31	6	15	24	40	25	17	19	20
Extra-marital affairs																		
Yes	64	73	60	76	53	74	47	51	73	54	91	67	57	45	61	71	63	71
No	34	23	38	20	44	24	49	49	24	44	7	32	40	52	36	29	35	25
Homosexuality																		
Yes	56	68	54	64	40	66	41	37	66	45	85	55	48	39	54	57	56	65
No	41	27	43	29	59	30	57	63	31	52	13	38	48	59	43	39	41	30
Euthanasia																		
Yes	64	75	60	79	54	74	51	42	74	53	91	66	56	48	61	76	66	66
No	33	22	37	20	41	23	45	54	22	44	9	31	40	48	36	21	31	30

which people believe these are 'religious' concerns, or, more probably, it may indicate the extent to which people's own inclinations agree or disagree with the advice they perceive the Church to be giving or that it would give on these matters. In the case of homosexuality, one explanation for a negative response when most of the others had been positive was, 'I think I know the advice the Church gives on that matter, and I don't agree with it'. (See Table 9.)

In general, men are much more in favour of the Church providing moral guidance on these issues than women, one of the few instances in the survey of sex-related differences. The widest spread between the two is on the issues of homosexuality and abortion, where there is a 20% gap between the two groups, but even on such a non-sex-related issue as euthanasia there is a 14% difference. Does this reflect the fact that women see the moral pronouncements of the Church on issues of private morality as those of a male establishment that has little understanding of their views and needs? It is certainly one of the results of the survey I least expected.

Among Christians, Nonconformists are most anxious for Church guidance (except on the issue of homosexuality) and Church of England least. Naturally, the results correlate positively with Christian commitment, although more than 50% of atheists believe the Church should give guidance on marriage and divorce and extra-marital affairs!

The two follow-up questions were, 'When the Church makes a stand do you think it influences the way you behave, or does it make no difference?' and 'Do you think it has any influence on society at large or does it make no difference?' The combination of results here I found rather amusing because, in general, people seemed to believe the Church's stand would make no difference to them personally, but that it was likely to influence society at large. One gets therefore a picture of people who want the Church to sound off on various issues not for their personal edification but because it may do some good to the 'others'. The authority of the Church is seen as a curb to the excesses of society at large, but not necessarily as a force overriding one's own sense of what is acceptable behaviour. Then too, given the high percentage of people who are convinced that they are already living in conformity with Christian morality, it may be that they feel any guidance the Church gives will be in line with their behaviour anyway and thus, to them, superfluous. (See Table 10.)

When asked the same question in relation to issues of public morality (poverty, ecology and environment issues, unemployment, Third World problems, racial discrimination, disarmament, and war), the response was again significantly positive overall, though there were greater differences depending on the specific issue. Here the perception of whether the issue was 'religious' or not was clearly relevant. In general, those issues that would be broadly perceived as having a clear religious dimension, such as poverty, racial discrimination, and Third World problems, gained a very high positive response (88%, 86%, and 85% respectively). Those not so perceived (ecology, war, disarmament, and unemployment) received correspondingly lower positive responses (68%, 69%, 61%, and 57% respectively). One wonders whether the response on the issue of unemployment might have been higher if the sample had included more people likely to be affected by it. Teachers were significantly more in favour of Church guidance on this matter than other groups (75% as opposed to 59% of professionals and only 38% of students).

None of the notable discrepancies between men and women that were present in the questions about private morality appeared here. Possibly women see the Church's stand on public issues as less personally threatening than that on private issues. There was again a positive correlation with church attendance, and Nonconformists once more were most anxious for Church guidance, with Roman Catholics next and Anglicans (except on ecological issues) least anxious. This would seem to dispel the notion that 'the Church' in England is seen simply as the established church or at least that its pronouncements are relevant only to those within the bounds of establishment.

When one proceeds to the two follow-up questions (whether the Church's pronouncements affect the actions of the respondent or society at large), the same curious paradox emerges – they have little or no effect on the individual answering the questionnaire, but he or she is convinced they are efficacious in society at large. What optimism!

Three key questions in this area tried to get beyond the

TABLE 10 *The Church's influence* (col. %)

	Total	DENOMINATION				BELIEF			RELIGIOUS UPBRINGING		RELIGIOUS ATTENDANCE				SCHOOLING			
		Cath-olic	C. of E.	Metho-dist	None	Chris-tian	Agno-stic	Athe-ist	Yes	No	Once week or more	Once month	Less often	Never	Church-den. state	Non-den. state	Church-aff. indep.	Non--aff. indep.
Total	614	60	350	76	94	385	142	78	332	281	161	87	192	174	371	70	93	79
When the Church makes a stand do you think it influences the way you behave, or does it make no difference?																		
Does influence	38	57	36	50	15	51	18	10	47	28	73	46	25	16	35	46	39	47
Does not make any difference	59	40	61	49	85	45	81	90	51	70	24	51	72	83	63	51	58	49
Don't know	3	3	3	1	–	4	1	–	3	2	3	3	3	1	2	3	3	4
And do you think it has any influence on society at large or does it make no difference?																		
Does influence	55	48	54	46	69	51	60	65	51	58	53	48	54	60	53	53	55	63
Does not make any difference	41	42	42	50	29	43	39	35	43	39	40	44	44	38	43	40	42	32
Don't know	4	10	4	4	2	6	1	–	6	3	7	8	3	2	4	7	3	5

'content' of morality to assess its nature as perceived by these people. The first was about absolute versus relative morality. Those surveyed had to choose between two statements: 'There are absolutely clear guidelines about what is good and evil. These always apply to everyone, whatever the circumstances' and 'There can never be absolutely clear guidelines about what is good and evil. What is good and evil depends entirely on the circumstances at the time.' A clear majority (62%) opted for the second statement, which proposed a relative morality rather than the absolute moral stance of the first statement. Students were particularly likely to opt for relative morality (75%), while professionals were least likely to do so (51%). Interestingly, this was one of the few instances where there were significant differences based on type of university degree – those who read science were considerbly more likely to take an absolute stand than those who read arts subjects (40% and 26% respectively). Possibly the study of science, at least at the undergraduate level, raises expectations of the possibility of absolutes, while the study of arts subjects undermines it. Those who identify themselves with the political right are also more likely to opt for absolute morality than those of the left, and it may be that there is some overlap here with science and arts graduates respectively.

At the same time, those with a degree or postgraduate training are less likely to believe in absolute morality than those with only diplomas, 'A' level, or 'other' – 30% for first degrees, 35% for postgraduate degrees, 41% for diploma/'A' level, and 59% for 'other'. It must be noted that the first degree and postgraduate results are the wrong way round for complete tidiness, but the general trend seems beyond dispute. Christians are much more likely to opt for the absolute moral choice than agnostics or atheists, and the more frequently they attend church, the more likely they are to do so, ranging from 57% for those who attend once a week or more to only 22% among those who 'never' attend. Nonconformists take an absolutist stand more frequently than Church of England or Roman Catholics. The latter produced the highest 'don't know' response – 8%.

These results would indicate that the highly-educated, secular élite, particularly those educated in an arts subject, increasingly reject not only the rigid moral teachings of the

TABLE 11 *Which of these statements comes closest to your own point of view? (col. %)*

	SAMPLE GROUP				SEX		SUBJECTS				QUALIFICATIONS				POLITICS		SEES LIFE AS	
	Total	Students	Teachers	Professionals	Male	Female	Sciences	Appl. Sciences	Arts	Vocational	Post grad.	Degree	Diploma/ 'A' level	Other	Left	Right	Meaningful patt.	Chance series of events
Total	614	205	214	195	388	226	159	88	188	198	136	319	141	17	253	298	357	183
There are absolutely clear guidelines about what is good and evil. These always apply to everyone, whatever the circumstances.	35	22	35	47	37	31	40	38	26	36	35	30	41	59	28	38	43	22
There can never be absolutely clear guidelines about what is good and evil. What is good and evil depends entirely on the circumstances at the time.	62	75	61	51	60	66	60	61	66	62	60	67	57	41	68	60	54	76

		DENOMINATION				BELIEF			RELIGIOUS UPBRINGING		RELIGIOUS ATTENDANCE				SCHOOLING			
	Total	Cath-olic	C. of E.	Metho-dist	None	Chris-tian	Agno-stic	Athe-ist	Yes	No	Once week or more	Once month	Less often	Never	Non-den. state	Church-aff. state	Non-den. indep.	Church-aff. indep.
Total	614	60	350	76	94	385	142	78	332	281	161	87	192	174	371	70	93	79
There are absolutely clear guidelines about what is good and evil. These always apply to everyone, whatever the circumstances.	35	35	35	41	17	44	23	14	39	29	57	32	29	22	36	33	33	33
There can never be absolutely clear guidelines about what is good and evil. What is good and evil depends entirely on the circumstances at the time.	62	57	63	58	79	53	73	85	57	69	37	66	69	76	63	66	58	61
Don't know	3	8	2	1	4	3	5	1	3	2	6	2	2	2	1	1	9	6

Church but the very idea of absolute moral teachings and values.

A second 'fundamental' question dealt with notions of human sinfulness. Here there were three options: 'All people are sinful by nature' (the orthodox Christian position); 'only some people are sinful' (a heretical view espoused by Pelagius in the early fifth century, and by numerous others since); and 'sin is a meaningless concept'.

Overall, more people (47%) agreed with the first, orthodox option than with either of the other two, and between them the results were fairly evenly divided with 22% opting for 'only some people are sinful', while for 24% 'sin is a meaningless concept'. There was a strong correlation between the results and Christian commitment, with 81% of those who attend church once a week or more believing that 'all people are sinful by nature', while only 26% of those who never go to church believe this. 43% of agnostics and 51% of atheists believe that 'sin is a meaningless concept' – hardly surprising since sin, whether or not meaningless, is certainly a *theological* concept.[1] Among Christians, Roman Catholics are most convinced of innate human sinfulness (60%), while Church of England adherents are least convinced (51%). Rather curiously, those from church-affiliated state schools are most likely to see all people as sinful, while those from independent schools (either church or secular) are least likely. This presumably ties in with the inclination of those from the former to a more rigorous self-examination, noted above. Church-affiliated independent schools produced significantly more people who believed 'sin is a meaningless concept' than any other of the four categories of school! Is this the end result of self-assurance and *savoir faire*? (See Table 12.)

What I found surprising in these figures is the large number of people who still do adhere to the traditional, orthodox position. The opening words of the baptismal service, 'Dearly beloved, forasmuch as all men are conceived and born in sin . . .' do seem to have their effect, probably because this is still the official position of all the major Christian denominations in this country. If one begins to look at individual cases, however, one finds that this is not universally so even within the ordained ministry.

I was so intrigued by the response of one ordained deacon

of the Church of England, who turned up in the survey as believing 'only some people are sinful', that I decided to do a follow-up interview. Under close examination, the person in question stuck to her guns and insisted that one could not possibly believe a newborn baby was 'sinful'. Was she aware that, despite a certain loose use of the word 'heresy' in ecclesiastical circles in recent days, this view might strictly be defined as heretical? Apparently not. The notion of innate sinfulness seemed quite unreasonable. Most people were *not* sinful – at least not compared with people who were *really* sinful like Hitler or Saddam Hussein. 'I certainly don't believe in original sin . . . I think there are some people perhaps who have allowed themselves to become sinful. We've got a choice in most things.' This rather worrying interview from someone recently trained for ministry and ordained in the Church of England raises real questions about how thorough and rigorous theological training for the ordained ministry is today. It is one thing deliberately to argue against Christian orthodoxy; it is quite another not even to be aware that that is what one is doing.

The direction in which this particular deacon is moving becomes much clearer if one looks at what now passes for 'orthodoxy' in some of the main-line churches of North America. At a recent baptism service in the United Church of Canada there was absolutely no mention of sin (original or actual). The parents promised to bring up the child in the Christian faith, and she was welcomed into the fellowship of the Church with the presentation of a rose (not a candle) – symbol of love, beauty, and, I should say, transiency. When I asked the officiating clergyman afterwards why, given this theological stance, he believed baptism was necessary, he replied that it was the welcoming of the child into the family of the Church which, of course, really begged the question. No, he did not believe in original sin if by that one meant depravity; one was born with the ability to do either good or evil.

This is Christianity without tears, Christianity in which the Bart Simpson translation of the Bible which simplifies 'grace' to 'goodness' will do nicely. There is no need to explain the concept of grace if there is no innate propensity to sin; grace is superfluous.

TABLE 12 *With which of the following statements do you most closely agree?* (col. %)

	SAMPLE GROUP				SEX		SUBJECTS				QUALIFICATIONS				POLITICS		SEES LIFE AS	
	Total	Students	Teachers	Professionals	Male	Female	Sciences	Appl. Sciences	Arts	Vocational	Post grad.	Degree	Diploma/ 'A' level	Other	Left	Right	Meaningful patt.	Chance series of events
Total	614	205	214	195	388	226	159	88	188	198	136	319	141	17	253	298	357	183
All people are sinful by nature	47	43	51	48	49	45	49	47	44	49	49	48	41	71	40	53	59	28
Only some people are sinful	22	17	23	28	23	22	20	22	22	27	21	18	35	12	19	25	22	23
'Sin' is a meaningless concept	24	34	20	18	23	25	26	25	27	18	23	27	20	18	32	18	15	44
Don't know	6	6	6	6	5	8	4	7	8	6	7	7	4	–	8	4	5	5

		DENOMINATION				BELIEF			RELIGIOUS UPBRINGING		RELIGIOUS ATTENDANCE				SCHOOLING			
	Total	Cath-olic	C. of E.	Metho-dist	None	Chris-tian	Agno-stic	Athe-ist	Yes	No	Once week or more	Once month	Less often	Never	Non-den. state	Church-aff. state	Non-den. indep.	Church-aff. indep.
Total	614	60	350	76	94	385	142	78	332	281	161	87	192	174	371	70	93	79
All people are sinful by nature	47	60	47	51	27	59	27	27	55	39	81	55	35	26	46	56	48	47
Only some people are sinful	22	13	26	30	14	23	23	18	21	25	10	21	33	23	26	13	24	13
'Sin' is a meaningless concept	24	17	21	11	55	11	43	51	18	31	4	15	26	45	23	23	24	32
Don't know	6	10	6	8	4	6	7	4	7	5	5	9	6	5	5	9	4	9

The final 'significant' question attempted to probe the nature of morality and people's beliefs about it. They were asked whether they believed Christian morality to be chiefly about right feeling (for example, loving one's neighbour) or right action (for example, not lying or stealing). The results here were very evenly divided with 37% opting for 'right feeling' and 34% for 'right action'. 27% insisted (perhaps rightly) on 'both' – an alternative not provided by the interviewer.

The division may appear to be an arbitrary one insofar as right feeling is only evident if it manifests itself in right action; and right action, in a majority of cases (though by no means always), will be motivated by right feeling. The intention was to try to differentiate between those who saw morality as a matter of externals, and those who were more concerned with 'the devices and desires of our own hearts'. All America laughed when Jimmy Carter said that he had committed adultery in his heart, but he was only applying to himself the strict standard of Christian morality set out in the Sermon on the Mount (Matthew 5.28).

One would expect that those who judged morality by actions would be more likely to believe that 'only some people are sinful', because many people succeed in living, for the most part, externally 'good' lives. Once one applies the internal standard, however, 'goodness' becomes immensely more difficult. This correlation does exist, though not as strikingly as one might have imagined. Of those who think morality is about right feeling 52% also believe all people are sinful as opposed to 47% overall. Similarly, only 44% of those who believe morality is about right action believe all people are sinful by nature, as against 47% overall. Those who believe sin is a meaningless concept are, appropriately, divided evenly between whether it is about right feeling or right action – 36% for each.

It may be that this is a specific example of the general difficulty of asking conceptual questions such as this in a survey. The responses are often instinctive and may not be thought out in a consistently logical pattern.

No direct attempt was made in the survey to discover what, specifically, these people regarded as 'sinful'. If one is to take the pronouncements of major Church figures – or at least the

TABLE 13 *With which of the following statements do you most closely agree? (col. %) (For each answer the upper line of figures is for those who see life as a meaningful pattern, the lower for those who see life as a chance series of events.)*

	Total	Right feeling	Right action	Both	Don't know
Total	614	37	34	27	3
All people are sinful by nature	47	52	44	48	32
		40	31	27	2
Only some people are sinful	22	21	27	20	16
		34	41	23	2
'Sin' is a meaningless concept	24	23	26	21	37
		36	36	24	5
Don't know	6	4	3	11	16
		24	19	49	8

pronouncements that are reported in the press (and I do recognize that they may not be precisely the same thing) – as a guide, the overwhelming concern seems to be with sexual morality. The headlines alone tell the story: 'Pope rails against the "sensual" West'; 'Dilemma of sex and the single Christian'. (The latter article, based on the recent Marc Europe survey, claims that 31% of their sample of teenagers, mostly committed Christians, believe pre-marital sex between unmarried people is acceptable.)[2]

Modern literature also encourages this narrow view of what Christian morality is about. The title of A. N. Wilson's *Incline our Hearts* is taken from the response to each of the ten commandments in the Book of Common Prayer communion service, 'Incline our hearts to keep this law'. But as Julian, the narrator, recalls the phrase in later life, he remembers it specifically with reference to the commandment concerning adultery, leading to the rather trite observation at the end of the novel that he doubts that this prayer will be fulfilled in him – at least with regard to this particular commandment. Even Jeanette Winterson's highly perceptive *Oranges are Not the Only Fruit*, while treating the brutality of religious fundamentalism in its various guises, concentrates largely on sexual taboos.

This narrow focus from both religious and secular sources emphasizes action rather than feeling and, more significantly, deflects debate about the fundamentals of moral behaviour. Could it also explain why so many students (36%) believe their actions in private life do *not* fit in with Christian morality?

The overall impression left by the answers to this part of the survey is that our morality is indeed broadly 'Christian', but that it is also largely unconsciously so. Judaeo-Christian morality in our society *is* morality, and we are brought up short when we encounter other religions, such as Islam, that incorporate different moral codes. We sometimes make the mistake of assuming their attitudes are 'immoral', even though they may spring from a more consistent and consciously thought-out set of premises than do our own.

There is a tremendous desire for the Church to take a moral stand on important personal and social issues (this role of the Church ranked third highest among the options presented), but a paradoxical unwillingness to follow those stands if they happen to disagree with what the individual previously believes. Society probably will (or should) be affected by the Church's stand on these matters, but how this is to be achieved if the individual is not affected remains unclear.

Overall there appears to be a great deal of uncertainty about theoretical and conceptual moral questions, and this should be cause for concern. Is it another evidence of the Church's failed teaching role, or do the new services, particularly that of baptism, in their desire for inclusiveness, blur the edges of theological statements inherent within them?

Speaking about the ASB, Stephen Darlington, organist of Christ Church Cathedral, Oxford, says that although one knows the intention,

> the notion is that somehow people are going to understand what they're talking about if they're speaking in a language that they use every day, but I . . . feel that the concepts remain as misty as they always have done and it doesn't matter if you use the word 'you' or 'thou' – it's not going to make any difference to your understanding of it.

Lord Runcie notes the Pelagian character of the ASB, perhaps thereby explaining some of the confusion of the deacon cited above: 'The ASB has a kind of Pelagian character; it's all tremendously effortless. "We are the body of Christ." '

Has the 'incomprehensibility' of the Prayer Book been replaced with a 'woolliness' in the modern rites? In any case, if one connects this uncertainty with the fact that a majority of people now opt for a notion of relative morality (which makes decisions more difficult, not easier), one gets a picture of a society where there is basic agreement about certain fundamental things that are 'wrong', but beyond that core large areas of disagreement. Further, there is no evidence of an agreement on methods by which concensus might be reached. Coupling this to the high priority given to 'fulfilling oneself' in the first part of the survey, one can envisage a state in which once the area of accepted values and taboos is further eroded (as it constantly will be if present trends continue), the current state of general consensus will break down and, while everyone will wish devoutly to have it re-established, they will want it done only on their own terms.

What we really value, and how we act is probably discoverable not from answers to surveys but from our actions: how we spend our time, how we spend our money, and how much of our time we spend making and spending our money. Looked at from the outside (if that is possible), ours is a consumer society, with 'growth' as a chief good and buying as an economic imperative.

Interviewed while still headmaster of Harrow, Mr Ian Beer waxed eloquent on the forces the young must battle, growing up in what he sees as a 'dishonest' consumer society.

> I am happier about the way in which the young today are trying to cope with the life that they are going to live than I probably have been ever before. What, however, I am extremely critical of is the older generation, who I think are dishonest. I think that they are making it very difficult for the young to grow up, and I think that on the one hand I want the young to respect the older generation, but the more I look at some of the older generation the more I have to say to the young, 'Well, I'm very sorry, but if you've got any sense, you'll realize how awful these people are.'

He elaborates on what he means by 'dishonest' by referring to things like newspapers, through which the young receive information.

> The newspapers, in my judgement, have devalued themselves . . . in the use of words. For example, 'a highly confidential report which will be discussed next week' – what does this mean? . . . Again . . . 'A Hamlet cigar is happiness.' Now a Hamlet cigar in my judgement could be pleasurable (I don't happen to believe it is) but . . . it certainly isn't happiness in my understanding of the English language.

He also speaks of

> the way in which the young are manipulated in terms of money and credit, the whole system of alcohol, cigarettes, drugs, the moral structure – how on the one hand the advertisements will give the young the impression they've got to be doing these things if . . . they're going to be grown up big men, whilst we, on the other hand, are telling them something different – the dishonesty . . . of selling motor cars which will do 120 miles an hour when in fact the law says you must only do 70.

He concludes, 'All I'm really getting at is that to be a young person today is difficult because the older generation have made it incredibly difficult for them. . . They want to respect their elders.' As for the elders, 'They're all competing madly to try and make certain that their income is higher than their expenditure and their surplus is high in order to please shareholders.'

These economic imperatives in our society, as Mr Beer realizes, have all the force of moral imperatives. The ubiquitousness of the advertising industry and its appropriation of religious music cited earlier is not accidental. It quite sensibly knows what the Church seems to have forgotten – that the motive to action is emotional. An advertisement uses every means at its disposal to 'move' us to desire and act. If it has appropriated some of the devices the Church has found effective in the past to achieve precisely that end, that just shows how clever its creators are. Ultimately, there is no separating emotion and desire, value and action, meaning and morals.

With this in mind, I have left the most significant correlations with all these moral questions to the last, because they appear to be illustrative of just these interconnections: the relationship between the responses to these moral questions and those about whether one perceives life as a pattern or a chance series of events. Over the whole range of moral questions posed, those who see life as a chance series of events are significantly less likely to opt for the response of traditional Christian morality. Given that these people are also more likely to be agnostic or atheist, or very loosely connected to the Church, I do not present this as a surprising result. What I wish to emphasize is the extent to which all these factors, including even the cultural issues discussed in the previous chapters, are closely interrelated. The survey shows certain measurable links between what one knows, what one believes, and how one acts.

Table 14 sets out the correlations quite clearly. Those who see life as a chance series of events rate the importance of the Church, and every one of its roles *except* those of preserving historic buildings and maintaining and passing on a good tradition of music, words, and art, less highly than either those who see life as a meaningful pattern or the population at large. And although they may value a good tradition of music, words, and art, they score significantly less well on all the questions connected with knowledge of it: religious writers, composers, and ability to quote either the Bible or the liturgy and to recognize passages from them.

In relation to the specifically moral questions, they are more likely than average to opt for the relative-morality stance (76% believe there can be no absolutely clear guidelines about what is good and evil as opposed to 62% overall), they are much less likely than average to believe that all people are sinful by nature (28% as opposed to 47% overall) and much more likely to believe sin is a meaningless concept (44% against 24% overall). They are less likely to believe the Church should give moral guidance on issues of either private or public morality, and considerably less likely to be influenced by any pronouncements it may make on these matters. But, rather curiously, they still are nearly as likely as the

TABLE 14 *How important do you think it is that the Church plays each of the following roles in Britain today?* (% across)

	Very important	Fairly important	Not very important	Not at all important	Don't know
Helping the poor and distressed					
Sees life as...					
Meaningful pattern	64	32	3	1	0
Chance series of events	39	45	13	2	1
Conducting marriages and funerals					
Sees life as...					
Meaningful pattern	60	32	6	1	0
Chance series of events	43	37	16	4	1
Moral and ethical guide					
Sees life as...					
Meaningful pattern	57	33	8	2	0
Chance series of events	28	42	21	9	0
Aiding individual salvation					
Sees life as...					
Meaningful pattern	49	37	10	4	1
Chance series of events	20	43	24	11	2
Commenting on social problems facing our country today					
Sees life as...					
Meaningful pattern	34	41	18	7	0
Chance series of events	17	42	28	13	0

Preserving historic buildings

Sees life as...

Meaningful pattern	28	40	22	10	0
Chance series of events	32	48	16	4	1

Maintaining and passing on a tradition of good music, art and language

Sees life as...

Meaningful pattern	16	40	35	9	*
Chance series of events	15	32	39	14	1

* Less than 0.5

TABLE 15 *Moral attitudes (col. %)*

	Meaningful pattern (357)	Chance series of events (183)
(a) **Which of these statements comes closest to your own point of view?**		
There are absolutely clear guidelines about what is good and evil. These always apply to everyone, whatever the circumstances.	43	22
There can never be absolutely clear guidelines about what is good and evil. What is good and evil depends entirely on the circumstances at the time.	54	76
Don't know	4	2
(b) **With which of the following statements do you most closely agree?**		
All people are sinful by nature	59	28
Only some people are sinful	22	23
Sin is a meaningless concept	15	44
Don't know	5	5
(c) **Do you believe the Church should give guidance on personal issues such as. . .**		
Marriage and divorce	84	62
Extra-marital affairs	73	50
Euthanasia	73	49
Abortion	71	46
Homosexuality	68	38
(d) **When the Church makes a stand, do you think it influences the way you behave, or does it make no difference?**		
Does influence	52	15
Does not make any difference	45	85
Don't know	4	0
(e) **And do you think it has any influence on society at large or does it make no difference?**		
Does influence	54	56
Does not make any difference	40	44
Don't know	6	1

entire sample to believe that the Church's pronouncements will influence society at large! (See Table 15.)

To argue any kind of cause and effect from these figures would be futile. What does emerge from them, however, is a picture of two distinct societies, one of which sees life as a meaningful pattern and, while not necessarily devout, has some knowledge of the Church, its teachings and worship, and holds broadly to traditional standards of morality. The other group, predominantly though by no means exclusively agnostic or atheist, has little knowledge of either the doctrine or worship of the Church, and in moral matters takes a much more individualistic approach, both eschewing guidance from the Church and ignoring it when it is proferred.

Some of these people apparently believe they are rationally setting their own moral standards. In answer to the question, 'what has been the greatest moral influence in your life?' five insisted on writing in 'myself' and one 'own conscience'. What these people believe to be the source of the 'self's' notions of morality (innate ideas?) is not revealed.[3]

Even within the 'Christian' responses to the question on chief moral influences, there is a strong individualistic emphasis. Seven people wrote in 'Jesus Christ', and one 'personal encounter with Christ'. Here again we see the influence of the fundamentalist branches of the Church which emphasize the authority of this kind of individual experience above that of the historic community of believers. While there is cause for optimism in the large numbers of people who do still nominally adhere to 'Christian' standards of morality, and the impressive quantity of those who wish to hear the Church speak out on moral issues, this is counterbalanced by a lack of precise and clear thinking on moral issues coupled with an increasing emphasis on the individual as the chief moral arbiter of his or her actions.

I am not suggesting that the notion of individual responsibility for action is bad or dangerous. On the contrary, it was one of the great gifts of the Reformation. I do suggest, however, that a situation in which the philosophical basis of moral decisions rests with the individual – and that in a society where, as we have seen, the influence of Christianity in the home, never mind in society at large, is in decline – is cause for concern.

One of the great debates in our society today revolves around whether wrongdoing is solely the responsibility of the person committing it, or whether social conditions are in part the cause of wrongdoing. The debate is at least as ancient as Thomas More's *Utopia*: can society ever be 'good' until all those composing it are good, or can social conditions be so engineered that goodness becomes easier and more desirable than evil? Those who argue the first position often begin by asserting that people (usually 'young people') have not been taught 'the difference between right and wrong'. But this assertion assumes that there is a common consensus about what is 'right' and 'wrong'. While the survey shows that this is still broadly true, the combination of a belief in relative morality and the individual as the arbiter of conscience means that such assumptions are increasingly vulnerable. Indeed, the 'privatization' of morality has profound social implications. Morality has always been primarily involved with people's rights and duties in a social setting. At its most extreme, the internalization of values leads to their disappearance, the completely amoral and individualistic societies in which humanity can only 'prey on itself like monsters of the deep', portrayed by Martin Amis (*London Fields*) in this country and Tom Wolfe (*The Bonfire of the Vanities*) in America.

How can one separate self-interest and self-justification? If every person is the arbiter of his or her own conscience and actions in a society that is increasingly pluralistic, how can society function? The implications of this and of the other aspects of the survey for the broader life of the country are the subject of the final chapter.

5

A CITY OF GOD?

That most glorious society and celestial city of God's faithful, which is partly seated in the course of these declining times . . . and partly in that solid estate of eternity. . .

St Augustine, *The City of God*

One of the ideas that has dominated Western thought for more than sixteen hundred years is that of a society that is not only politically and socially a unity but also united under God. Visions of the heavenly Jersualem coalesced with the vast reality of the Roman Empire (and subsequently with the memory of it) to produce an ideal that found its classic expression in St Augustine's *City of God*. Of course, it never existed in reality – not in the so-called Holy Roman Empire, not in the England of Henry VIII despite the coincidence in one person of the head of Church and state, certainly not in present-day America with its coins proudly blazoned 'In God We Trust'.

What is new in the present day is not that this unified city-state has ceased to exist but that we have ceased to desire it. Why, if it never was anything more than a chimera, should this matter? Because our lives and societies are shaped as much by those things we dream of and strive towards as by those things we accomplish. The form of the epic did not cease to influence European writing during the long years that no one (Petrarch, Tasso, Spenser) despite effort, managed to write a successful one; its influence ceased when writers no longer *wanted* to write epics, when they no longer imagined that this was the literary ideal by which posterity would judge them. Similarly, the idea of the City of God is only now ceasing to influence the kind of societies we are shaping today.

The relationship between Christianity and secular society

or the state has been ambivalent from the beginning. The inherent conflict between the two was implicit in Jesus' oft-quoted 'Render unto Caesar the things that are Caesar's and unto God the things that are God's' – the first enunciation of the principle of the separation of Church and State.

But if early Christianity was initially seen as over and against the world, in the centuries following Constantine this perception changed. In Augustine's own thought there is still a necessary tension between the temporal city of God and the eternal one, and it is the latter that must be the true aim of every Christian. Throughout the Middle Ages, however, this tension lessened, and Christianity and the state came to be seen as, if not synonymous, at least mutually necessary for each other's preservation. The notable historical exceptions – the papacy at Avignon, the conflict between Becket and Henry II – were seen as cataclysmic events. Throughout most of its history, the Church has preserved an uneasy balance between that of critic and supporter of the state – a balance seen recently at its most precarious in the official service following the Falklands War.

Increasingly, however, in recent years the functions of Church and State have become separate. Particularly during the Thatcher years the Church was frequently rebuked for interfering in areas that were seen to be none of its concern: housing policy, unemployment, decisions about war and peace, and so on. It was told firmly by politicians to get on with the business of 'preaching the gospel' and 'saving souls' and to leave the affairs of this world to those elected to deal with them.

When the three contenders for the Conservative Party leadership were questioned about their religious beliefs, the replies (at least as reported in the press) seemed to show they didn't really understand what was being expected of them. John Major deflected the question to speak about 'living by those instincts and values that you think are important' – a response calculated to encourage individualism and subjectivity. He was quite happy that the Church should play a part in the political arena, but it should display a 'dispassionate sense of values'.[1]

At the same time, the established Church is coming to resent the ability of parliament and the prime minister to affect important appointments and to have the power of veto over certain matters decided by the Church's own synod. The very structure of the Church is essentially foreign to the structure of the secular world in which it finds itself. If hierarchy (as I have argued) is so deeply embedded in Christianity as to be a part of doctrine, not just practice, this poses particular problems in the practical realm of church government. Traditionally hierarchical, it is now, through its synods at various levels, incorporating some of the apparatus of democratic government, but the fusion of the two can be an uneasy one. Lord Morris thinks that 'to be a Bishop is to be one of the most uneasy men in the world . . . because one half of your mind is saying, "I must obey God and interpret the Word to everybody"; and the other half is saying, "Well, what do most of you think? Is there a consensus? There is? Thank God for that. I don't have to exercise my authority!" '

At a more practical level, we have seen that of those surveyed a very high proportion believed that it was important for the Church to enter the public arena in such areas as 'helping the poor and distressed' and, giving guidance on issues of public morality such as poverty (88% overall). Yet faced with the more general question as to the importance of 'commenting on social problems facing our country today' only 29% rated it 'very important'. Is it possible that these people, like the state itself, want the Church to act as a benign helper at the social level, but do not really want hard criticism of fundamental principles of public policy?

What is indisputably true is that political leaders no longer need to be Christian in order to be elected, and that Christian principle is no longer one of the chief factors in government decision-making just, as we have seen, it is no longer a chief factor in voters' judgements about the government or voting intention. Peter Berger would see this as an example (though by no means the most extreme) of a 'global tendency . . . [to] a state emancipated from the sway of either religious institutions or religious rationales of political action.' He goes on to speak of those ' "antiquarian" cases in which the same political secularization continues to be decorated with the traditional symbols of religio-political unity, as in England or Sweden'.[2]

The use of the word 'decorated' is provocative. Is it also

just? Presumably Berger is thinking here of the ceremonial side of the Church's role, such as the archbishop turning up to the state opening of parliament, which the former arch- bishop saw as legitimate and important – a genuine way of uniting the secular and the sacred. On the other hand, Lord Rees-Mogg sees the role of Archbishop of Canterbury as increasingly 'peripheral' and 'impossible', and this impossi- bility is directly linked to its established position. 'It is possible to be a good Chief Rabbi; it's probably possible to be a good Archbishop of Westminster. . . It is *not* possible to be a good Archbishop of Canterbury. One can't really conceive what that would be'.

The concept of religion as 'decoration' may also point to an explanation of the puzzling phenomena noted in the previous chapter of people who want the guidance of the Church on moral matters, who believe their actions in private and public life are in conformity with it, but who do not consciously take a Christian perspective into account in their actions and who are unlikely to be influenced by the advice of the Church when it is proferred. Do we want the comfortable feeling that we are Christian people and a Christian society without the trauma of ascertaining whether this is genuinely the case?

The union of Church and State on matters of morality is a very comfortable thing, and there have been times in the history of the Church of England when its critical role has disappeared almost entirely, when the popular perception of 'the Tory party at prayer', has had a large element of truth. The looser association of Church and State today means that the Church is freer to take stands in opposition to government. But this is only relative. It still has an actual legal connection with the state and, through the representation of its bishops, at least a theoretical moral one.

The price the Church of England pays for being a state religion is not just the perception that it is still linked to an 'establishment' but the fact that its members are on average less committed than those of non-established denominations. The survey shows consistently that those respondents from the Church of England are less likely to be committed Christ- ians than either Catholics or Nonconformists. This is probably due not to a general lack of commitment among Church of England worshippers but to the fact that any state church becomes a respository (or depository) for those who have not quite decided they are agnostic or atheist but are in no sense practising Christians. 'Church of England' is what you fill in on your hospital form when confronted with the embarrassing question, 'Religion?' and lack the guts to reply 'None'. Even today, however, its position remains very different from that of the other denominations in England.

It has always been easier for these non-established faiths to function as critics of society, though more difficult for them to get a hearing when they do so. Their membership is on average more committed because it is composed of people who have consciously chosen to belong to that particular denomination; to be a Nonconformist is to have *chosen* not to conform. It is easy to belong to a state church; it is more difficult to belong to groups outside the mainstream, even in these days of religious toleration. And ease or difficulty in belonging to any group is one of the key factors in whether the membership is committed or not. It would be wrong to say that establishment encourages lack of commitment, but it does seem to make it more likely.

The arguments for establishment, however, are impressive. The Church 'over against the world' may produce a more devout band of adherents, but it is less likely to influence society as a whole. The large number of people in the survey who said the Church should give guidance on moral issues, and who rated the role of the Church as a 'moral and ethical guide' as third most important (after 'helping the poor and distressed' and 'conducting marriages and funerals') shows that its public function is valued. Many non-Church of England adherents – and not just those of other Christian denominations but atheists, agnostics and those of other faiths – claim they would regret the passing of establishment because they believe it would undermine even further the tentative agreements we still share about standards of morality. Jonathan Sacks in his 1990 Reith Lectures, said 'Disestablishment would be a significant retreat from the notion that we share any values and beliefs at all', and affirmed society's need for 'a moral and cultural base'.[3]

Significantly, what he actually said in full was that a *plural* society needs 'a moral and cultural base'. And herein lies the difficulty. The City of God, either in this world or the next, did not assume a plural society. Quite the reverse. Today we have a plural society whether we want it or not; it is no longer a matter of choice. Again Jonathan Sacks, determinedly optimistic, claims that pluralism and a religious society are not incompatible. He envisages 'a community of communities',[4] a collection of individuals with different religious beliefs still adhering to an over-arching system of values to which they can all subscribe.

This may well be possible for a religion such as Judaism which does not seek converts and does not make any claims to exclusive truth. But what of Christianity that does (though with increasing tentativeness) seek converts, and at least traditionally has claimed an exclusive truth leading to eternal life?

Dr Sacks' position also assumes that, broadly speaking, our moral codes are the same. This latter is not entirely true even of religions that share such a similar heritage as Christianity and Judaism. For example, wealth, which in the Old Testament and in present-day Judaism is seen as a sign of God's favour and blessing, has always been looked upon with suspicion by Christianity. The established church had difficulties with certain aspects of 'Thatcherism' that seemed to pose no problems at all for many of Mrs Thatcher's own constituents in Finchley. And once one broadens the perspective to include the many religions that are represented in present-day Britain, one finds that such matters as equality, sexual roles, and even the taboo on individual retribution are not the universal values we naively imagine. Eighteenth-century rationalism, that believed universal principles of conduct could be discovered by all civilized people, has fallen victim to the multiplicity of codes adhered to by people in England today, all of whom believe they are both 'civilized' and 'reasonable'. When the Church seeks to speak out, as Archbishop Carey has to City businessmen, it is accused of not understanding 'the realities of the situation', a statement that ties in with the lack of belief in any moral absolutes revealed by the survey.

In the face of this onslaught, we have adopted values that I would describe as 'soft' rather than 'hard' – soft not in the sense of easy, but soft in that they are general rather than specific and open to multiple interpretations. 'Tolerance', 'pluralism', 'multiculturalism', are some of these values. They are designed to give an ideal framework to what is already a social *fait accompli*, to foster peace and harmony in a society that is no longer held together by an authoritarian union of Church and State. They are given lip-service by nearly everyone living in England today including most Christians. They are, however, quite incompatible with any notion of an exclusive religion or one true path to eternal life. Instead their whole thrust is towards making life here and now tolerable.

Against this stand certain Christian denominations of a fundamentalist cast who believe that conveying the essentials of Christianity (as they perceive them) is of such paramount importance that it overrides the paler virtues of tolerance and plurality. And if anyone thinks such attitudes no longer exist outside the 'lunatic fringe' of American television evangelists, I would refer them to one of the mushrooming Evangelical branches of the Church of England in London where I recently heard in a sermon the following: 'Tolerance is the great virtue of our day. "It doesn't matter what you believe as long as you believe something." This thinking is anathema to Jesus and it comes from the Devil.' It is the combination of attitudes like this with the Decade of Evangelism (whose full implications are uncertain) that strike fear into the hearts of those of other faiths.

This raises difficult issues for the Church, particularly in its established form. What the Evangelical preacher was saying was wholly consonant with much traditional Christian doctrine. It would have been understood by Luther, Calvin, and the Catholics of the Counter-Reformation alike. And, incidentally, if you do genuinely believe in the eternal salvation or damnation of the human soul based on either deeds or faith in this life, then a number of things otherwise reprehensible, including the Spanish Inquisition, begin to make a lot of sense. It would not be approved of, however, by the broad tradition of the Church of England in this country, and certainly not by the prevailing secular ethos. The decline of a belief in hell already noted, 'one of the great changes that has come over Christianity,' according to David Edwards, and one which we underestimate, is linked to this movement from 'hard' to 'soft' options and values. 'Phrases like "necessary to salvation" no longer mean, I think, that if you don't accept that particular doctrine you are going to hell, which they *did* mean in the past.' The Church has yet to sort out fully what, in the present situation, it is 'saving' people from – or for. Elements in the Church, as for example the Evangelical clergyman cited above, are clear about this, but there is no concensus. There is no longer even a concensus about whether the focus should be on enabling people to live a fuller, richer life here and now, or whether this is a happy by-product of living a life that is a preparation for life hereafter.

In this situation, it may be fortunate that the great virtue of the Church of England has always been its comprehensiveness, its tolerance of diversity. Indeed, it has been suggested by some (notably David Edwards in his book *The Futures of Christianity*) that it is precisely this that the Church of England has to offer to other denominations and to the world-wide ecumenical movement. It is almost as if the Church of England had been preparing for the secular age before it arrived and had already found a means of legitimizing its demands under the umbrella of Christianity. The bitter experience of the Civil War at home in the seventeenth century and the diversity of cultures abroad to which the Church of the Empire ministered were jointly responsible for a breadth and tolerance unusual in religious practice.

Today it is natural to accept these standards as the norm – so much so that anything else has come to seem bad manners at best and madness at worst. If we are to have a 'state' religion in a society where large minorities are non-Christian and many of those who are Christian are only nominally so, it might be felt one could hardly do better than what we have now. Similarly, this experience of diversity and tolerance makes the Church of England a natural leader in world ecumenical councils.

Against this, one can set the words of Charles Gore, Bishop of Oxford at the beginning of this century, who claimed that established Christianity,

> whether in the civilised Roman Empire or in half-barbarous tribes or in modern nations, the sort of Christianity which claims to embrace the whole of society, which it costs nothing to profess and into which children are baptised practically as a matter of course, appears to be as audacious a departure from the method of Christ as can well be conceived.[5]

It is widely acknowledged that one of the directions in which the Church in general is moving is towards an increasing secularization of its message, which may lead to the deliberate excision of all or nearly all 'supernatural' elements from the religious tradition[6] – and of which the baptism in a Canadian United Church described in chapter 4 is presumably one example.

At the opposite extreme, contemporary thinkers are very much aware of the dangers of fundamentalism. There are the examples of the 'Holy Wars' abroad and the Salman Rushdie affair at home. A. N. Wilson's diatribe *Against Religion* bases its argument on precisely this aspect of it – religion is by its very nature intolerant, even murderous. Jonathan Sacks devoted an entire Reith lecture to the modern rise of fundamentalism, which he sees as relatively benign as long as it remains private, but terrifying when it merges with the state and nationalism. 'It is one thing to believe in absolute truth; something else to seek to legislate it in a plural culture.'[7]

In all of the above, it seems that we are faced with choices between a strong, fundamentalist individual belief, versus a flabby, modernist collective faith that is compatible with the other ideals of modern society.

If these are genuinely the alternatives they pose a difficult problem for the Church, because implicit in them is a choice between a 'this world' role and a salvationist stance. The survey indicates that among most people this choice has been made; they have opted for a 'this world' role. In a homogeneous society, the 'city of God', the choice does not arise because the good of the individual and the good of society are synonymous. But in a pluralist society, while many Christian values such as loving one's neighbour, helping the poor, doing good to one's enemies, are certainly 'good' for society at large since they are compatible with an uncritical tolerance, other scriptural injunctions such as 'go out into the world and teach all nations, baptizing them in the name of the Father, and of the Son, and of the Holy Ghost', clearly are not.

What appears to be happening at the moment is that Christianity in England has divided not so much along denominational lines but along these other lines of choice. Thus we have the mainstream of the Church of England emphasizing social values (the report on the inner cities and the related Church Urban Fund is one recent example), while outside this inoffensive orthodoxy groups exist, often formally attached to these churches, purveying a quite different message – one of the need to be 'saved', to be 'set apart'. The Decade of Evangelism, which should unite these two groups, has raised a sense of deep unease, probably because of the recognition of the inherent incompatibilities I have set out. Attempts to disarm this concern may illustrate ways of bringing the message of Christ to an essentially secular world with some sensitivity, but they do not really address the problem of 'conversion' in a society that contains a large element of people from other religions. With regard to Judaism, for example, we have had Richard Harries, Bishop of Oxford, denouncing any 'hard campaign of conversion' and the Revd John Fieldsend of the Church's Ministry Among the Jews claiming that it is offensive for the Church to be told that it should not try to share the gospel with Jewish people.[8]

Related to these divisions, but distinct from them, is yet another – that between those who believe it is the pure, unvarnished truth of the gospel that will win people, and those who emphasize the need to 'package' Christianity so that it is attractive and palatable to those currently outside the Church. John Irvine, priest-in-charge of St Barnabas' Kensington, a highly successful 'planted' church, takes the former view. When I asked him to what he attributed the very large congregation he now has in the formerly dying parish, he answered unhesitatingly, 'I would say that the simple answer is that where the true gospel is preached boldly and with relevant application, there will be those that respond.' Unlike Don Cupitt, he does believe in Truth with a capital 'T'. 'Personal conviction is very important, but it's secondary to Truth itself. It's no good being personally committed about the wrong thing.'

Increasingly, however, the Church seems to be concentrating on *how* it attracts people rather than what it attracts them to or for. All these injunctions to 'communicate', to present Christianity to 'modern man' emphasize the *how* rather than the *what* of the Christian message. There has been a recognition within the Church for a long time that the peripherals are important in 'getting people involved'. As Lord Morris succinctly put it, '[The clergy] are quite contented to judge a man by his works not by his faith, and especially a woman, if she comes along and cleans the brass and makes the cakes and sweeps the floor, then she's a *very* committed Christian. Nobody would *dare* ask her if she believed in the resurrection of the dead.' But the current emphasis on the externals makes it seem at times that the Church is going the route of the political parties who rely more and more on 'presentation' and less and less on substance.

Most worrying of all is the fact that these matters are not openly or cogently debated within the Church. Indeed, clergy seem often to live in such enclosed compartments of Christianity that they do not even realize they *are* matters for debate. At a recent clergy discussion about why people might come to church, one incumbent said, as if it were the most obvious answer in the world, that they came, of course, so as to be able to make a choice between heaven and hell in an afterlife. He was as astonished to discover that not all his fellow clergy shared this view as they were to find that he held it.

In the face of all this, Norman Tebbit's tongue-in-cheek suggestion that religion, like everything else in Britain, should be privatized, comes to sound less than wholly crazy. The Church then can propound whatever nonsense it wishes but with no implication that its views have any official sanction. It may collect its followers wherever it can, provided they pay their dues because, like everything else that is privatized, it will seek to turn a handsome profit. If the present dilemma of the Church arises from its being less than wholly integrated with society, could its total divorce from the mainstream of English life provide a cure?

If the conviction of a small but strong band of believers is the prime goal, than this might indeed work – though it is equally possible that a 'privatized' church might become less, not more, a church of conviction in an effort to attract more followers and hence more profit. If meeting the needs of humanity and society at large is the goal, however, then this is obviously not a solution to be contemplated.

Here we return to some of the questions posed in earlier chapters. Ignoring the question of what God may want for society at large, what does society at large itself *really* want? On the one hand, we have a vision of life free of preconceived patterns, free of imposed notions of sin and the need for redemption. We have post-eighteenth century men and women finally emerging into complete freedom, arbiters of their own actions, creators of their own patterns. This attractively open-ended scenario to human life is what I understand writers such as Margaret Drabble to find appealing. This is the optimistic way of looking at our situation.

There is another, which starts from the same premise – that we are living in a postmodern, post-Christian era – but perceives this as apocalyptic rather than millennial. These philosophers and thinkers point to values determined by the dominant consumerism of the post-industrial era. They argue that we have already left the point at which our values were directed to something outside ourselves, and are rapidly moving beyond the point where they are largely self-fulfilment (the modernist stance) to those of simple enjoyment and self-indulgence (a postmodernist stance). At the heart of this life they see not endless, open-ended opportunities but vacuity.

The results of this survey would seem to indicate that on one level people share the optimistic view – they want freedom, open-endedness, they see 'fulfilling themselves' as the chief goal of life. Alongside this, however, they want patterns, they want meaning, they want a life that 'goes somewhere'. They seem unable to cope with the very freedom they most desire. And in the absence of Christianity or other religions they have found in this century secular alternatives that fulfil the same function – Marxism, Freudian or Jungian psychology, or nationalistic religions such as fascism. One could argue that the passion with which various popular movements such as disarmament and the green movement have been espoused in the last few decades is indicative of a religious vacuum waiting to be filled. 'Man' may well be a 'worshipping animal' as Enoch Powell asserts; what he sees as shackles may be essential to his very existence. Scientific knowledge can never be a complete substitute for religion because science is 'fragmentary and incomplete; it advances but slowly and is never finished; but life cannot wait. The theories which are destined to make men live and act are therefore obliged to pass science and complete it prematurely.'[9]

Against the evidence for the need of religion in the individual must be set the enormous indifference to religious questions of any kind in large numbers of the population as shown in the survey. Asked to rate how important God is in their lives on a scale of 1 to 10, those who said 'not at all important' (17%) were outweighed by those who said 'very important' by only 1%; the mean score overall was 5.52. From responses to other questions, it would seem that it is not that many of these people have consciously rejected God and religion, but that they have never thought seriously about the matter at all. Moyser's assumption that 'death sets firm limits on secularization'[10] simply may not be true. Of those surveyed 88% either 'strongly agree' or 'tend to agree' with the statement that 'Death is inevitable, it is pointless to worry about it'. The tendency in our society is to treat death as something to be ignored rather than to be prepared for. Doctors 'save lives'; they never 'postpone death'. We are brought up short when Tom Stoppard, after the murder of one of his characters on stage, has another quip, 'It's not as though the alternative were immortality.'[11]

If the signals from the private sphere are mixed, when one turns to the need for religion in the public sphere there are different, though no less prevalent, ambiguities. Firstly, there is debate as to what creates a strong, cohesive society. Is it shared values and beliefs, or are economic factors more important? Or is there another alternative: can there be values and beliefs that are not merely 'weak' so as to incorporate diversity but 'strong' in the sense that they make a virtue of that diversity?

It is the assumption of the latter possibility that must be at the heart of the 'pluralist', multi-cultural society. This assumes that tolerance and diversity (and tolerance of diversity) are not simply 'goods' but can be emotive forces sufficiently strong to bind together a nation.[12]

As a theory this has much to recommend it. If a way of life that is increasingly a pragmatic necessity can also be legitimized as an ideal, nothing could be more satisfactory. Much evidence, however, indicates that this is unlikely to occur. Pluralism and tolerance are 'cool' values. That is, they are perceived to be admirable but not emotive. People may die for freedom, but who will die for pluralism?

Further, all the contemporary evidence shows that states are held together by precisely those old-fashioned values so frequently denigrated as no longer of importance – language, ethnic culture, a shared history, and common religion. The dramatic break-up of larger conglomerates – most notably the Soviet Union, Yugoslavia and Czechoslovakia – and the threatened separation of French from English Canadians are prime examples.

The situation in Canada is an admirable illustration of the general point. The economic advantages of union are blatantly obvious, and there are emotive arguments as well. Much newsprint is consumed portraying the wonderful vista of a country of great diversity and wealth stretching from sea to sea. Yet for many people it remains somehow theoretical, remote. What really matters is the language one speaks, the songs one has sung from childhood, the landscape one has grown up with. These are the things that have the power at an emotional level to move and bind together as individual groups the French Canadians, the Indians, the Inuit, and even the English Canadians. Against this, all the economic arguments in the world, and all the chatter of pluralism, tolerance, and diversity are weak.

England is a vastly different case, because until recently it has been a relatively homogeneous society bound together, despite the much-discussed class distinctions, by a common language, religion, and common assumptions about right and wrong – the very characteristics that appear to make for a cohesive, stable society. Suddenly this is no longer so. The survey deliberately excluded those in the population that belong to other faiths, but even among those who are or might in theory be Christian, there is a great diversity of attitudes. A general lip-service to Christian morality is undermined by the responses to the more searching questions and a general uncertainty about fundamental philosophical and theological questions dealing with relative and absolute morality, innate sinfulness, the basis of morality, and so on.

The cultural elements of Christianity, as we have seen, have disappeared or are rapidly disappearing. Where they still survive they are divorced from their two sources of real power: from their original context on the one hand and from those in whom belief preserves their original meaning on the other. Neither the incorporation of Tallis motets into advertisements as background music nor the aesthetic appreciation of Taverner masses by a small musical élite will 'save' these things in any live form. Their survival in these limited ways seems to be a concrete example of Eliot's dictum about having the experience but missing the meaning or, in the case of the intelligentsia, *understanding* the meaning without assenting to it.

In this fragmented situation, what will bind the country together against a rampant individualim that is implicit in the survey results and explicit in many observable aspects of present-day England? Nationalism which, to use Berger's word, uses religion as a 'decoration' still seems to have some power, particularly in time of crisis as the Gulf War and the Falklands conflict illustrated. But outside these arenas, nationalism itself now often wears a tongue-in-cheek aspect, a last-night-of-the-Proms stance, aware of its own anachronism and incipient absurdity. For if within an individual country such as Britain nationalism and pluralism are quite compatible, pluralism in its larger manifestations is inherently hostile to nationalism of any variety. Even nationalism may not be the reliable ally of stability that it was once believed to be.

So what can one advocate that will satisfy both the needs of the individual and the good of society? A return to the past is not an option. Our current values and way of life have been so deeply shaped by the combination of Enlightenment and the Industrial Revolution that we would have to undo centuries of intellectual history and economic 'progress' to restore a unified Christian culture, comparable to that of the Middle Ages where, 'only the church reigned supreme, not the state, economic production, science or art. The transcendental values of the Gospel might encounter worldliness, hedonism, sensuality and violence, but it was not confronted by competing ideals, a secular culture that would have been independent of the church and capable of creating an autonomous order.'[13] What has been thought cannot be forgotten; what has been created in terms of economic structure cannot be dismantled, even if Berger's assessment that religious beliefs inevitably lose plausibility in urban industrial society, not because they have been converted to some other ideology but because no ideology can take root in such a situation proves to be true.[14]

Modern society *has* certain values, but they do not necessarily add up to an ideology because they arise largely out of pragmatic economic realities rather than out of theoretical ideals. Growth, and its corollaries of 'progress' and scientific advance are built into the economic system. Individual fulfilment is a logical partner of capitalism. Egalitarianism and pluralism, while not economic necessities, become desirable in the wake of modern methods of communication which have created the 'global village'. To negate these values – and many one would certainly not wish to negate in any case – one would need to return to a whole pre-industrial society which, at the most basic level, would be incapable of feeding the present population levels of even the developed countries. On the other hand, to have them as our *only* values, to confuse values that have arisen out of historic and economic necessity with a value system, a complete and uncritically accepted ideology, is a serious mistake.

One alternative is to accept that since the public domain is largely given over to these values imposed by circumstance, the only room for ideology as such in modern society is therefore in the private sphere, the family. But the family itself is an increasingly frail institution and, as the survey has shown, people *want* religion to have a public role as well as a private one. The values of secular society cannot answer the predicaments that are inherent in human experience. Thus Daniel Bell in *The Cultural Contradictions of Capitalism* refers to 'the wheel of questions that brings one back to the existential predicaments, the awareness in men of their finiteness and the inexorable limits to their power . . . and the consequent effort to find a coherent answer to reconcile them to the human condition.' He argues that 'since that awareness touches the deepest springs of consciousness . . . a culture which has become aware of the limits in exploring the mundane will turn, at some point, to the effort to recover the sacred.'[15]

If this is indeed possible, what role can the Church play in assisting this 'recovery of the sacred'? It is easy to begin with the things it should *not* do. It should not assume that 'ordinary' people are incapable of sophisticated thought and that therefore meaning must be packaged in see-through plastic wrap and marketed in TV-ad size bites. It should not seek to sell itself in certain ways because it believes they have 'contemporary appeal': it does, after all, seek to embody the eternal amidst the transient. It should neither reject the past nor treat it as an antique shop to be raided for certain items of choice window dressing. It should cease to confuse help and kindness with condescension.

What it *should* do is above all to take seriously its prophetic and teaching roles. It should expect the highest standards of both its clergy and its laity in these areas. It should recognize that worship is a matter of the emotions as well as the understanding and that excellence in words and music (whether ancient or modern) is not incompatible with sincerity. Above all, it should attempt, through intellect and inspiration, to acquire and impart wisdom. Not the simplistic certainties of the television evangelists, but the complex results of an engagement of mind and heart in serious debate on those questions with which people still struggle. *Do* sorrow and suffering have place within a larger pattern? What is the chief purpose of life as we live it? Is there any point in thinking – if not worrying – about death?

The Church should become the street corner on which we can stand and witness the pattern of our lives and of humanity at large unfold. It will not be a medieval street corner, and the pattern may have complexities and ambiguities undreamt of by a medieval audience. But a genuine engagement with theological issues (and I am not speaking here of a quick course in comparative religion) should restore to us something of the assurance of the City of God without the (now unacceptable) social structures that originally sustained it. It should restore to us an ideology out of which values like tolerance grow naturally instead of being separate ideals, exalted to ideologies in their own right. In time it should produce a public ethos that is not superimposed on the private but rather a natural growth out of it; public values and morality should become the private writ large.

All this may be much too optimistic. My dominant impression in dealing with the survey results and the follow-up interviews was that most people had not so much consciously rejected Christianity's values or decided to abandon its literature or music but that these things have not been presented to them, the questions have not been asked. At the end of a long follow-up interview, the atheist professional, cited in chapter 1, said, 'Well, maybe now I will think more about these things'. This seemed a fitting conclusion.

NOTES

CHAPTER 1   THE IDEA OF ORDER

1. The 'mean' score is the average of the responses ranged from 5 (strongly agree) to 1 (strongly disagree); + 3 is neutral (neither agree nor disagree). Therefore any rating *below* 3 indicates some measure of disagreement with the statement, while any rating *above* 3 shows a corresponding measure of agreement. Some other questions as, for example, those rating the importance of various possible roles of the Church, are rated on a scale of 1 to 4, with 4 indicating 'very important' and 1 'not at all important'. The higher the mean score, the more important the role is judged to be.

The heading 'Methodist' is a general shorthand for Nonconformists and includes various other denominations such as Baptists, United Reformed, and fringe Evangelical groups. However Methodists do, as it happens, comprise by far the largest portion of this sample.

2. 'Individualism and the Intellectuals', *Culture and Society*, ed. Jeffrey C. Alexander and Steven Seidman (Cambridge, 1990), p. 225.

A more jaundiced view of the meaning of self-fulfilment comes from Lord Morris of Castle Morris: 'If you dig rather deeper . . . into what self-fulfilment means, I think in many cases among the intelligentsia you will find that like King Lear they did ever but slenderly know themselves, and there is no depth to that. That is a cult phrase. . .'

3. William Crashaw, *The Complaint or Dialogue, betwixt the Soule and the Bodie of a damned man* (London, 1622).

4. *The Sunday Times*, 23 December 1990.

5. Don Cupitt, *Taking Leave of God* (London, 1980), p. 166. An amusing, if rather cynical view of this philosophy comes from one of Don Cupitt's former colleagues at Cambridge whom I interviewed: 'Discarding all the clever bits, you can say what he's saying is Christianity is morality plus calming yourself down and so forth, you know, having a nice cup of tea and sort of relaxing.'

6. *Taking Leave of God*, p. 145.

7. *Taking Leave of God*, p. 155.

8. Alasdair MacIntyre, quoted by David Jenkins in *God, Miracle, and the Church of England* (London, SCM, 1987), p. 97.

9. Margaret Drabble, *The Radiant Way* (London, Penguin, 1988), p. 298.

10. Margaret Drabble, *A Natural Curiosity* (London, Penguin, 1990), p. 176.

11. Mary Tannen, 'Devil's Thumb', *The New Yorker*, 4 February 1991, p. 33.

12. Nicholas Mosley, *The Times*, 26 September 1991.

13. *Culture and Society*, p. 218.

14. Max Weber, 'The Protestant Ethic and the Spirit of Capitalism', quoted in *Culture and Society*, p. 221.

15. Stephen Hawking, *A Brief History of Time* (London, 1988), p. 175.

CHAPTER 2   CUSTOM AND CEREMONY

1. C. Geertz, 'Religion as a Cultural System', quoted in *Religion and Ideology*, ed. Robert Babcock and Kenneth Thompson (Manchester, 1985), p. 67.

2. Geertz, p. 74.

3. Roger Ascham, *The Schoolmaster*, ed. R. J. Schoeck (Toronto, 1966), p. 101.

4. David Martin, 'Personal Identity and a Changed Church', *No Alternative* (Oxford, Basil Blackwell, 1981), p. 12.

5. I. R. Thompson, 'Gospel Message/Gospel Manifestation', *No Alternative*, p. 23. Expanding on this theme, Lord Morris says of the liturgical revisionists, 'They understood that words *mean* certain things; they never understood and still do not understand that words *do* certain things – not just mean.'

6. Quoted by Thompson, *No Alternative*, p. 29.

7. Alice Munro, 'Age of Faith', *Lives of Girls and Women* (New York, 1974), p. 83.

8. Only 57% of those who went to church-affiliated independent schools claim to have been brought up religiously at home – slightly more than the 51% from non-church-affiliated schools, but significantly less than the 71% from church-affiliated state schools. This shows that the religious element is a much more important factor in choosing a church-affiliated state school than a church-affiliated independent one, and this difference must be borne in mind in interpreting all other comparisons between these two types of school.

CHAPTER 3   CHRISTIANITY *OR* CULTURE

1. Penelope Lively, *Judgement Day* (Harmondsworth, Middlesex, Penguin, 1982), p. 5.
2. John Donne, *Sermons*, ed. G. R. Potter and E. M. Simpson (Berkeley, 1953–62), iii, 56.
3. Susan Howatch, *Scandalous Risks* (London, Collins, 1991), p. 65.
4. David Hare, *Racing Demon* (London, Faber, 1990), p. 87.
5. *Independent on Sunday*, 13 January 1991.
6. *Good News in Our Times* (London, Church House Publishing 1991), p. 11.
7. *Good News in Our Times*, p. 12.
8. The following argument is not intended to apply to those living in totally alien cultures. I do not subscribe to the view that African tribes must learn to sing common metre Anglican hymns in order to enter the Kingdom of Heaven. But unless we accept the total alienation of some elements of English society from others, one surely must accept that what may initially be unfamiliar can and should become familiar.
9. Charles Bremner, *The Times*, 17 May 1991.
10. Penelope Lively, *Moon Tiger* (Harmondsworth, Middlesex, Penguin, 1988), p. 57.

CHAPTER 4   MORALS AND MEANING

1. Janet Daley, in an article printed in *The Times*, 6 September 1991, concerning the riots in Newcastle, succeeds in arguing for the inherent predisposition to evil in human nature without ever using the term 'sin'.
2. *The Times*, 19 June 1991.
3. For a detailed and perceptive account of the effects of individualism and emotivism in ethics, see Alasdair MacIntyre, *After Virtue* (London, Gerald Duckworth & Co., 1981).

CHAPTER 5   A CITY OF GOD?

1. *The Times*, 26 November 1990.
2. Peter Berger, 'Social Sources of Secularization', *Culture and Society*, p. 240.
3. Jonathan Sacks, '1990 Reith Lectures: 4', *The Listener*, 6 December 1990, p. 18.
4. Sacks, '1990 Reith Lectures: 6', *The Listener*, 3 January 1991, p. 9.

5. Quoted in Peter Cornwell, *Church and Nation* (Oxford, Blackwell, 1983), p. 18.

6. Berger, *Culture and Society*, p. 246.

7. Sacks, '1990 Reith Lectures: 5', *The Listener*, 13 December 1990, p. 11.

8. *The Times*, 30 March 1991.

9. E. Durkheim, 'The Elementary Forms of the Religious Life', reprinted in *Religion and Ideology*, ed. Robert Babcock and Kenneth Thompson (Manchester, 1985), p. 52.

10. George Moyser, 'Patterns and Trends', *Church and Politics Today* (Edinburgh, 1985), p. 18.

11. Tom Stoppard, *Jumpers* (London, Faber, 1972), p. 52.

12. This is the reverse of the 'melting pot' theory of the United States where the initial diversity was supposed to have as its end a unity 'under God', and a common adherence to the ideals enshrined in the Declaration of Independence.

13. Ernest Troeltsch, quoted by Wolfgang Schlucher, 'The Future of Religion', *Culture and Society*, p. 255.

14. Cited by R. Babcock, 'Religion in Modern Britain', *Religion and Ideology*, p. 228.

15. Daniel Bell, 'Modernism, Postmodernism, and the Decline of Moral Order', *Culture and Society*, p. 328.